The Ride-Alongs

WHAT I LEARNED ABOUT POLICING, CRIME, AND THE NEW YORK CITY JUSTICE SYSTEM

BRANDON STEINER
with **C. L. STEINER**

Disclaimer: This book is a truthful recollection of actual events in the author's life. Some conversations have been edited and/or supplemented.

The book includes some personal views and opinions of the author and does not necessarily reflect the positions or opinions of any other organization, institution, or individual. The content presented herein is based on the author's perspective and interpretation of the subject matter. Neither the publisher nor any associated parties shall be held responsible for any consequences arising from the opinions or interpretations expressed within this book.

Published by:
Brandon Steiner
SCARSDALE, NY

Copyright © 2025 Brandon Steiner

ISBNs
979-8-9986235-0-9 (softcover)
979-8-9986235-1-6 (hardcover)
979-8-9986235-2-3 (ebook)

Photo on page 99 reprinted with permission of the New York Adventure Club.

*This book is dedicated to my wife, Mara,
my son Crosby and his wife Nikki,
my daughter Nicole and her husband Trevor,
my son Keith Martinez and his wife Alyssa.
Everything I do is dedicated to them.*

Contents

Introduction: Trading in Sports for the Squad Car, 1

1. The Four-Six • *Bronx, New York*, 7
2. The Four-Six • *Night Two*, 17
3. The Three-Two • *Manhattan*, 25
4. Community Leader Russell Smith • *Harlem*, 32
5. The Seven-Three • *Brooklyn*, 39
6. The Seven-Seven • *Crown Heights, Brooklyn*, 44
7. Community Leader Lisa Kenner • *Brownsville*, 48
8. A Small City Comparison • *Syracuse, New York*, 56
9. Intermission • *Connecting the Dots*, 68
10. The Academy • *Part One*, 72
11. The Academy • *Part Two*, 89
12. The Crime Lab, *Part One—Guns*, 101
13. The Crime Lab • *Part Two—Drugs*, 119
14. The Courts • *Part One—The Judge*, 126
15. The Courts • *Part Two—The Public Defender*, 135

16. Underground • *The Times Square Subway Hub*, 144

17. Managing the Masses • *The Strategic Response Group's Crowd Management Unit*, 151

18. The Takedown • *Full Circle with the Four-Six*, 159

19. A Civilian's Conclusions • *My Two Cents*, 167

Acknowledgments, 181

About the Authors, 183

INTRODUCTION

Trading in Sports for the Squad Car

I'm a businessperson. My primary business is sports. I've been in the sports memorabilia business for decades and sports marketing even longer. I founded and ran Steiner Sports for many years. Most recently, I founded Collectible Xchange, a platform for collectors and athletes to buy, sell, and trade their memorabilia.

For years now, I've had the privilege of working with the New York City Police Department to improve morale in several police stations by bringing in well-known athletes for meet-and-greets, redecorating meeting and muster rooms (the gathering points for officers to learn of their assignments before they go on patrol) and helping out in any other way I can.

My first contact with the NYPD was several years ago when K. C. Fuchs, CEO of the Silver Shield Foundation, which provides support for families who have lost loved ones in the line of duty, contacted me about the 44th Precinct in the Bronx. The officers and staff there needed morale support after losing two of their people. One, an officer named Dennis Guerra, had been trapped in an elevator during a fire and died from smoke inhalation; the other, Kalyanarat Ranasinghe, a seventy-one-year-old civilian employee on traffic-enforcement detail, died after being hit by a truck.

A room we redecorated at the 32nd Precinct,
featuring a wall of officers' favorite athletes.

Police precincts remind me of my old fraternity—these are people who spend so much time together, and death has a profound effect on every member of the team. It's not like what you see on television. The precinct staff was devastated, and we did what little we could to help out. Yankee Stadium is in the 44th Precinct. I've done a lot of work with the New York Yankees over the years, and I've developed relationships with many current and former players. I set up a luncheon with Reggie Jackson, so the officers and families could spend some time with a famous Yankee. Also, Reggie felt an affinity with the Four-Four, because as a player, 44 was his number.

Looking around the precinct house, I saw active and involved men and women—uniformed officers, plain-clothed detectives, and dispatchers—handling waves of calls, a revolving door of responding to the unknown. These people spent most of their waking hours, some for more than thirty years, within the building, and as I looked around, the age and staleness of the building were a stark contrast to the warmth of the "family" that worked inside it. This workplace, frankly, was dismal. The precinct house needed more than a lick of paint; it needed a décor as inspiring as the people in it. I decided to come back and redecorate the precinct. Once we got permission from the precinct commander (he was pretty enthusiastic about it), we worked on the common room first, where police and community meet. We wanted that space to be warm, bright, and friendly for everyone who entered it.

As a businessman, I know that you're only successful if your patrons feel connected with the purpose of your service or product. Similarly, I thought the members of the community, who are not customers but taxpayers who are served by the police, should feel more invited and connected to the missions of the precinct in their neighborhood.

With this in mind, we decided that, while redoing one precinct was good, it wasn't enough, so we went on to redecorate four other precincts. I saw how deeply involved these cops are in the community, and I wanted to learn and understand what actions we could take to help the police and the communities they serve.

During the COVID-19 lockdowns and subsequent protests, I thought about safety and community. How can we close the gap between the police and the community? So many people were moving out of the city I grew up in, one of my favorite cities on the planet, and safety was the number one issue they cited for leaving. I knew one thing: You can't solve a problem until you understand the problem.

The news wasn't really giving me answers. Depending on

which voice you heard, the cops were worse than criminals or the protesters were violent crazies. I wanted the truth and to see for myself. I wanted access—to ride with cops to see what they saw. I contacted several people in the police department, but I wasn't exactly at the top of their inbox. I wasn't hearing back from anyone. The breakthrough came after I requested permission to ride along with officers from the New York City police commissioner at the time, Keechant Sewell. In return, I received an invitation to be the keynote speaker at an NYPD Leadership Conference. Of course, I accepted. Fortunately, both the commissioner and the deputy commissioner were there.

After my leadership speech (which was pretty good, by the way), the incoming commissioner gave me his contact information and asked me to keep in touch with him. I restrained myself from contacting him too soon to ask permission to ride along and record my experiences so I could write this book. Usually, permission for a ride-along is a one-shot deal, but I knew one ride-along wouldn't give me more than a glance at cop life. So, I asked for what I believed I needed, which is one of my tenets for success in business: ten to fifteen ride-alongs over a few months. This number could give me a broad enough view of what goes on between police and the community in the city. The department was kind enough to give me what I asked for.

My wife thought I was crazy. She absolutely forbade me from embarking on this project. Mara is a brilliant woman, but since she once told me to get a job instead of starting Steiner Sports, I sometimes take her advice with a grain of salt.

Then, my adult son and daughter voiced their opinions, which were very close to my wife's. Now it was three against one. I believe in always listening to other people's opinions, especially those who care most about me. After I listen, I give those opinions careful consideration. Then I do what I want.

TRADING IN SPORTS FOR THE SQUAD CAR

I wanted to know what it was like to face danger. Cops live with risk constantly and experiencing that level of jeopardy would give me greater empathy and context for what these officers go through.

I never knew that kind of peril. I grew up in Brooklyn, but not on what you would call "the mean streets." My neighborhood was Jewish and Italian. Black kids were bussed in from East New York. Nights weren't always quiet, but they featured yelling out of windows to come home for dinner instead of screaming in terror and the occasional car backfire instead of gunfire.

As I grew older, I explored more of the city and got to know a lot of Manhattan and the part of the Bronx that surrounded Yankee Stadium. But I didn't hang out in dangerous neighborhoods. Today, I live in the suburbs. I realized that I'd been out of touch with the city I love.

> You can't become closely acquainted with anything from afar or through the lenses of other people. I needed to get in a car, patrol the streets, see with my own eyes the interactions that have been polarizing for as long as I've been alive.

You can't become closely acquainted with anything from afar or through the lenses of other people. I needed to get in a car, patrol the streets, see with my own eyes the interactions that have been polarizing for as long as I've been alive. In the ride-alongs, I'd spend sufficient time with people who deal with the most trying life-and-death situations. I wanted to learn the principles they use to size up a situation, prioritize its importance, strive to bring every encounter to a successful conclusion under high-stress circumstances, and make decisions in the blink of an eye. I also wanted to witness when or if they fell short.

Support the police? Defund the police? Who are the good guys? What goes on in the streets? And why? Before getting involved in this project, I was like most people in America: I couldn't even grasp the arguments.

Someone told me long ago that if you're going to be part of the game, you have to know the rules, know the players, and be in position. I had no natural desire to be in this game, but as a citizen and taxpayer, I needed to understand.

This journey takes us to five precincts and offices throughout three of the five boroughs of New York City, on ride-alongs in some of the roughest neighborhoods in town. I went to visit a small city in Upstate New York to see how different policing was there, if at all. I spoke to community leaders and activists, as well as lawyers and judges, to understand where the judiciary fits in. I learned all I could. Now, I want to share that knowledge with you to increase awareness of how policing works.

And here we go.

CHAPTER 1

The Four-Six · *Bronx, New York*

> *Violence across New York City is uneven, while some parts of our city feel like havens, others continue to feel like war zones, including parts of my district.*
> —NEW YORK CITY COUNCILMEMBER PIERINA SANCHEZ[1]

In my suburban town, about an hour's drive outside Manhattan, about 100 people are arrested each year. Only four of those arrests are for violent crimes.

In 2022, the Bronx's 46th Precinct had about 2,200 violent crime arrests. The "Four-Six," as it's called, contains the Fordham, University Heights, Morris Heights, and Mount Hope neighborhoods. It's only one square mile, but home to 200,000 people. For perspective, that's 100 times the number of people per square mile in nearby Westchester County, where I live. The Four-Six is known as "The Alamo" because it has a reputation as a Wild West war zone. *Time* magazine once called this neighborhood "the most dangerous square mile in America."

---

1 Office of the Mayor, "Mayor Adams Announces Pilot Program to Improve Quality of Life in Persistently High-Crime Areas, Root out Causes of Systemic Violence and Disorder." NYC.gov, December 9, 2024, https://www.nyc.gov/office-of-the-mayor/news/905-24/mayor-adams-pilot-program-improve-quality-life-persistently-high-crime-areas-#/0.

On the afternoon of July 14, 2023, I stood in the locker room of the 46th Precinct, strapping on a bulletproof vest and a windbreaker with the word POLICE emblazoned across the back. I had one thought going through my mind: *What the hell am I doing?*

A week earlier, Inspector John Potkay, commanding officer of the Four-Six, called me and said, "Brandon, we've got your first assignment. It's a good one." Then he told me that the night before, the Fourth of July, they'd had a shooting and an overturned car. That was in the first ten minutes. "I think there'll be a lot of action for you in this precinct," the inspector said. I'd been to the 46th Precinct before. In 2017, after respected officer Miosotis Familia was shot and killed while on duty, we wanted to help with morale at the precinct. We renovated their muster room with a vast mural of the Alamo mission in San Antonio. We also took the crew to a Yankees game.

So, there I was in body armor and a police jacket, waiting to get into a car with officers Adrian Vasquez and John Dailey. We'd spend the next eight hours patrolling "The Alamo." And I couldn't shake the thoughts: *I'm going into one of the most dangerous neighborhoods in New York City—maybe the entire country—where people get shot.*

We would be patrolling the neighborhood from 4 p.m. to midnight. Being a typical sweltering summer in the Bronx, kids and adults were opening fire hydrants everywhere. That's one more problem, not only because it decreases the water pressure for fighting fires but also because much of this neighborhood is built on hillsides. If the hydrants keep spraying, stores and basement apartments at the bottom of the hill will flood. So, cops have to go around shutting off the hydrants, which just get opened up again.

I had no idea what to expect when I got in the back of the car behind officers Vasquez and Dailey. It was still daylight, and I could see that the car's exterior was reasonably clean, which surprised me since these cars are in almost constant use. On this July night in the broiling Bronx, I was grateful for the air conditioning. There was a cage between the officers and me, which served as a constant reminder of where I sat. I hoped that if they arrested someone, they would put them in another car and not next to me.

I asked, "So when you guys get out of the car, what do I do?"

"You come with us," Vasquez, who was driving, said.

Then Dailey added, "Everywhere, stay one foot behind us."

The radio between the two officers chattered often. Not nonstop, but regularly. One thing I would learn quickly was the high level of communication between the officers I was with, the dispatchers, and the other officers on patrol.

We headed out, and the first thing that struck me was how small an area the precinct covers. If you want to picture what one square mile looks like, get in your car and drive a mile, turn right, drive a mile, and do it again until you've made a square. So, whatever's in that box is one square mile. And 200,000 people live in that box, which comprises the Four-Six. In that one square mile, there are twelve gangs. There are 200 police officers assigned to the precinct, down from 280 over the past four years. Every precinct is down in personnel between 25 and 30 percent since 2020.

Cops aren't sitting around. These officers work hard, and they're not overstaffed by any means. How do 200 cops, over three different shifts, deal with the problems and situations of 200,000 citizens in one of the most dangerous parts of New York City? What I learned was that, just like it is in business, everything boils down to two principles: prioritization and communication.

Every one of us makes decisions about what things are important and then prioritizes what's most important. Every yes decision is a no to something else. Police officers must make those decisions in a finger-snap instant.

> Every yes decision is a no to something else. Police officers must make those decisions in a finger-snap instant.

I saw a circle of people standing on the corner, a mix of men and women ranging from their teens to fifties. "What's going on over on over there?" I asked, trying not to gawk from behind the window of the back seat of the car.

"Oh, those guys? They're selling drugs."

"Are you going to do anything?"

"It's not that simple," Vasquez replied, his hands loose on the wheel. "We know what they're doing, but we'd have to see a transaction taking place in order to move in. There's another crew of officers that goes around to try and defuse some of the obvious dealing, so that's not really our focus. We step in when necessary, but as you can see, that kind of dealing is happening on many corners."

As we turned the corner, I saw a group of tough-looking young men just hanging out, watching the street.

"What's going on over there?"

Officer Vasquez answered, "That's a gang spot."

"You mean they're always there?"

Officer Dailey nodded.

"Do they have guns?" I asked.

"Some of them might have guns," Dailey replied.

"In any street situation, how do you know when to step in?" I asked, as the officers cruised by the gang spot. Most of the young men ignored us, but a couple gave us hard looks.

Dailey responded, "We have to prioritize every situation. Some people are double parked. Some are smoking weed. Some are smoking crack. We need to assess and prioritize each situation and the circumstances around it."

I noticed ordinary citizens sitting in front of their buildings. It was a summer evening. They were talking, laughing, playing dominoes . . . and ten yards away, some skinny guy was slinging dope.

I wanted to know about the disconnect between the ordinary workaday citizen and the gangsters on the street, so Officer Vasquez told me about two kids who got shot a couple of days earlier over a "drill rap." Drill rap is a subgenre of gangsta rap with aggressive lyrics about shooting, killing, and revenge. It's dark and violent. There's a level of drill rap about disrespecting another gang member or members who got killed. This "music" fuels conflict between gangs.

"An eighteen-year-old, who was a relatively good kid, does a rap that disrespects a gang member," Vasquez began. "The gang member shoots the kid's friend in the leg and then shoots the kid in the thigh, hitting an artery. So, two kids get shot, and one dies—over a stupid insult song."

> There's a level of drill rap about disrespecting another gang member or members who got killed. This "music" fuels conflict between gangs.

I'm told this happens all the time. A dozen gangs all hate each other, and they randomly (and often) shoot at each other. YGs—young gunners—try to make their marks by shooting people, often without any reason.

On the street, the intensity of friction was palpable. I don't know if it was the skeptical looks we were getting from the young gangsters or the story Officer Vasquez told me, but I was scared to death. There was not one minute in the eight hours of my ride that I could think, *Oh, this is normal, this is cool.* I could see that, at any moment, something crazy could happen.

I did notice that the entire time of my ride-along, Dailey and Vasquez were in constant communication with Central and the other patrol cars in the area. At any point, if something shifted and we needed help, backup would be there. Somehow, this didn't reassure me.

I was still full of fear. I did not feel comfortable or safe. But I had signed up for it.

"How do you guys handle this?" I asked. "I mean, you might not be afraid, but obviously there's danger here. How do you deal with not feeling safe?"

"Look," Dailey answered, his head straight ahead, mindful to not take his eye off the street, "this is one of the most difficult precincts to police, and we get used to it."

"Every day is a different day," added Vasquez.

Neither one had answered my question, but I didn't press.

I saw areas where there was a police car stationed at a particular corner, just parked there all night, with the cops inside watching the scene. And right in front of them were individuals who, while I don't know exactly what they were doing, I could tell weren't doing the right thing. And Vasquez and Dailey explained to me that with recent changes to the law, like the end of the city's stop-and-frisk policy and increased paperwork, it was harder than ever to arrest someone, even people they knew who had sheets with twenty or thirty prior arrests.

The Calls

Besides patrolling for crime, calls from Central need to be answered. Every time someone calls 911, police have to go to the source of the call, find the person or persons who made the call, and fill out a report. That's every single call. Sometimes, they can't even find the caller.

How do cops prioritize everything they have to do?

One of the calls during my ride-along involved an accident between a motorbike and a car. A simple accident takes police time—interviewing, getting each party's account of what occurred, writing a report that insurance companies often ignore—effectively taking two cops off the street for an hour.

These streets in the Four-Six are also overrun with motorcycles, mopeds, electric scooters, and homemade vehicles. They're not licensed; kids ride without helmets, go the wrong way down one-way streets, and ride on the sidewalk. Should cops stop every rider to give them a ticket? Every ticket written means potentially half a day in court to defend the ticket if the person receiving it does more than ignore it. They can confiscate an unregistered vehicle, but they've taken so many that now they're running out of space to keep them.

A radio call came from 911 Central—a 1030, a robbery within the past five minutes. Officer Dailey picked up the handset and confirmed receipt of the call. We needed to go to the homeless shelter where a woman called to report a robbery. We arrived at the shelter and found the caller waiting for us outside. She said her girlfriend stole her money and her phone. This domestic dispute was now a crime because the woman had reported it as a robbery. Whether or not they reconciled, the suspect, if caught, would be arrested for robbery.

The next call was really scary—a 1052 DV.

"Are there weapons involved?" asked Dailey.

"Unknown," the dispatcher answered.

A 1052 DV is a domestic violence call; the dispatcher said a kid was screaming in the background. The radio squawked as another car told us they would back us up at the address.

"Why did you ask about weapons?" I asked.

They told me about an occurrence in another precinct where two officers entered a similar apartment and were ambushed and killed. Not what I wanted to hear.

We climbed the stairs of an apartment building until we reached the fifth floor. As instructed, I remained a foot behind. It was an old pre–World War II apartment building from the days when people with money lived in the neighborhood: thick walls, huge apartments.

Dailey knocked on the door. The door opened, and the woman in the apartment motioned for us to come in. "No, ma'am," Dailey said. "Tell us what's going on here."

We saw from the doorway that it was an enormous apartment with three or four bedrooms, and with the amount of stuff in every corner, it looked like an entire family was living in each bedroom. We wouldn't be walking into an apartment with a few people in it; we'd be entering an apartment with as many as fifteen to twenty people.

We heard kids screaming, and the woman who opened the door began to speak in rapid-fire Spanish, and we were not going in because the officers couldn't assess the scene. Vasquez radioed for instructions, and we waited until a superior told him to cautiously enter the apartment.

There was a man in the apartment wearing an ankle monitor, indicating he was out on bail or parole. Vasquez and Bailey asked questions to determine if a child was being abused in an apartment full of people and, between the kids screaming and the adults talking loudly, a cloud of noise. All I could think was that there were more of them than us; we had no backup, and I couldn't understand what any of the adults were saying. Fortunately, Vasquez was fluent in Spanish.

Finally, the woman brought a child of about eight or ten to the front door, and he looked fine—clean, well fed, no bruises, not crying. Dailey questioned two of the adults, asking how many people lived in the apartment, what did they see, and how many children were there. Meanwhile, Vasquez talked to the boy to determine if there was anything real going on, and eventually, they determined that there was really nothing terrible happening.

By the time we left the apartment building to go back to the car, it was dark outside, which I found disconcerting. No sooner did my heart rate return to normal did the next call come—a 34 in progress (an assault)—in a housing project called "the Towers." I kept quiet on the way there.

These two buildings, River Park Towers, are the tallest in the Bronx, and they are swarming with gangs, reeking of drugs, and seething with danger. There's a narrow driveway between the buildings, and once you drive in, you can't turn around, so there's only one way out. Couple that with the darkness of night, and I felt more vulnerable than I ever had.

We drove past a group of young men standing around in the dark—even though I could hardly see anything but shadows. People were walking back and forth between the buildings—like a cop movie and a zombie movie spliced together. The officers assured me that they hated coming to this place. These buildings are enormous, over thirty stories tall, and these cops were probably almost as scared as I was.

"One of the issues here," said Dailey, "is that we have no idea how many people live in each apartment."

"It's not like one family per apartment," Vasquez explained. "Some of these apartments have eight or ten people living in them." I'd already seen earlier how many people can cram into one apartment.

In the structure of the NYPD, the Police Service Areas serve Housing Authority developments as opposed to precincts. It's still the NYPD; there's no separate housing police department anymore, but the jurisdictions differ.

As often happens with a call to the Towers, four police cars responded. Somebody punched somebody in the face. Our car wasn't the responding unit. We were backup. I was standing next to the building with four or five cops, waiting to see what, if anything, was going to happen. One officer told me that I needed to take a few steps away from the building because people may start throwing bottles, batteries, or an air conditioner out of their windows at us.

"What?" I was confused.

"Usually, it's a chair or a bucket of water," Dailey said plainly, "but I've had an air conditioner thrown at me. We don't know which apartment it could come from. In any case, you need to take about five steps back."

I hadn't done much besides watch and listen, but I noticed that, as my adrenaline level dropped, I was exhausted.

Two other officers entered the building and, after about fifteen minutes, came out with a man in handcuffs. We got back in our car and left.

It was close to midnight, and I was more than ready to go home. I realized my shirt was stuck to my back, probably from the nervous sweat. Back at the Four-Six, I shook hands with Vasquez and Dailey and shuffled to my car. I hadn't done much besides watch and listen, but I noticed that, as my adrenaline level dropped, I was exhausted.

CHAPTER 2

The Four-Six · *Night Two*

The safety of the people shall be the highest law.
—Marcus Tullius Cicero, Roman Statesman

Eleven days later, on July 25, 2023, I was back in the Four-Six, and it took me about that long to decompress from the first ride. In the moments when I had time to think, I found myself going over the experiences of that first time—my fear, the confidence of the partners I'd been with, and the way they had interacted with people in the neighborhood.

There were still so many things I wanted to know. How does it feel to know that the job is bigger than you, that you can't solve all the problems? How do these officers prioritize without knowing all the variables? And every answer brought more questions.

Officers Vasquez and Dailey were off that night, so I was assigned to ride with different teams of two partners each. Precinct Commander Inspector John Potkay established a schedule for me. Commander Potkay was in charge of the station, and that evening, he was also in charge of moving me around among patrol cars.

The shift began at 4 p.m., and like my first ride-along, I'd be back to my car by midnight. On the first part of the shift, I sat behind Sergeant Rubin Seijas, who had been on the force since

2013, and Officer Anthony Lombardo, who had two years on the job. Seijas was driving, and this car was a little more beat up than the first car I rode in.

Sergeant Seijas, Officer Lombardo, and me before our shift began.

At first, things were pretty quiet. We drove around, getting to know each other. Then, a call came in about a knife situation; a woman in an apartment was threatening someone. That was all we knew.

On the scene, we learned that the fracas started when some young guys were ringing doorbells and running away. I don't know why men in their twenties were engaged in juvenile behavior like that, but these guys rang the wrong doorbell. A woman had come to the door with a knife and told him she'd use the knife if they came to her door again.

Seijas and Lombardo assessed the situation to determine if there was an actual threat. I thought about the excessive number of 911 calls. One after another, and so many didn't seem to be emergencies. But I learned from Sergeant Seijas that every single call must be taken seriously because what looks like a minor issue now can explode later.

> I thought about the excessive number of 911 calls. One after another, and so many didn't seem to be emergencies.

"Shots fired! Shots fired!" we heard through the radio. Another patrol was calling for backup.

Seijas floored the accelerator, and I found myself pushed against the back seat as they sped and straddled the middle of two-lane streets. The siren blared; the lights flashed like dizzying strobes. I held on to the door and closed my eyes to keep the nausea at bay.

What the hell am I doing here? was my first thought. I didn't say a word. I wanted the officers to concentrate on swerving around parked cars and running red lights. More questions swirled in my mind, but I didn't dare interrupt the drive. *Is there a shootout going on between two gangs? A hostage situation? A kid with a gun shooting up the street?*

Seijas floored it on the Grand Concourse (a major Bronx thoroughfare) and pulled up onto the sidewalk about twenty yards past the entrance to the location where the shots had been fired. I should have offered to stay in the car, but with adrenaline flooding through me, I got out of the vehicle.

Officer Lombardo stood in the street; I stood frozen beside him on the curb. Suddenly, a black BMW 4 Series jetted out. Beyond just speeding—it was rocketing. The Beemer missed hitting Lombardo by under six inches, which means it nearly hit me, since I was shadowing him.

Is this the guy who did the shooting? There was no way to know.

Back in the car, we chased the BMW, along with another police car. We made the last high-speed turn and realized the driver was going to the hospital. He pulled up in front of BronxCare, formerly Bronx Lebanon Hospital. The driver had the guy who'd been shot in the car. He pulled the victim out and carried him through the emergency department doors.

The two officers in the other police car got out to meet the driver of the BMW as he exited the ED. They began pushing each other and yelling, and Lombardo and Seijas stood by to see if they needed to intervene.

The driver of the BMW claimed he got a call to take his friend to the hospital. The cops didn't believe him (security cam footage later showed that he was lying). The BMW driver had three other passengers, each with a rap sheet featuring multiple priors.

Sergeant Seijas decided we should go into the ED and talk to the gunshot victim. We entered and learned from the doctor that the victim was bleeding out of his gut. Although the man would most likely live, we were not granted access to him at that time.

Outside the hospital, the driver of the BMW had been detained by the officers in the other car. Another car had arrived, and I met Captain Rebecca BukofzerTavarez, who explained that because there had been a shooting, detectives were on their way to open an investigation. There was nothing more uniformed officers could do.

Should we go back to the crime scene and look for evidence to pick up? Witnesses to interview? No, a detective unit was already on the way to do those things. We hung around while the detectives tried to get as much information from the driver as possible.

Later that evening, Captain BukofzerTavarez showed me

the video. A guy on a moped rode by a van, out of which drugs were being sold, and opened fire, and one bullet hit one of the guys in the van. The shooter was unknown. His reason for shooting was also unknown. *Disgruntled customer? A resident fed up with dealers? Local competition?* Who knew? They had a clear picture of the shooter on the scooter and would utilize it to identify and track him down.

Motorbikes, mostly unlicensed, are popular in the city. Their versatility enables them to ride on sidewalks, squeeze into back alleys, and ride against traffic and one-way streets, making them harder to catch once they flee a crime scene. That's exactly what happened with this shooter.

Being at the hospital made it a good time to transfer me to another car with two new officers. The adrenaline surge I had experienced during the high-speed ride began to subside. I felt wrung out.

How do these guys do it, going from a domestic call to a shooting, then to a robbery, all in the space of an hour? I, on the other hand, am completely exhausted with hours to go in the shift.

Captain BukofzerTavarez had said something to me earlier that I was just beginning to understand.

"A cop has to be a counselor, an enforcer, a scout, a decision-maker, a diplomat, and a lot more besides."

"Every cop in the Bronx understands that they're never going to fix the enormous problems that are going on in the Bronx," she said, "but the real difficulty is that the scope of the police officer's job is so broad. These guys look for situations your everyday citizens train themselves to avoid. Police officers have to take all kinds of abuse from all kinds of people. A cop has to be a counselor, an enforcer, a scout, a decision-maker, a diplomat, and a lot more besides."

After Dark

Central called in with a robbery. A guy pulled a knife, stole a woman's necklace, and ran away. We were racing again.

All the officers could do for the woman was take her statement.

In the car, we turned the corners of the one square mile of the precinct and spotted a vehicle two cars in front of us with blacked-out windows—not tinted, but pitch black, which is illegal in New York.

We waited for the car, which was signaling a left turn, to make the turn. Instead of making the left, the driver ignored the "NO U-TURN" sign in front of her and made an illegal U-turn!

The officers sounded the siren, pulled the car over, talked to her for a bit, and let her go with a warning.

"You've got someone with illegal window tinting who just made an illegal turn, and you're not even giving her a ticket?" I asked.

"Discretion is a fine line," one of the officers explained, "and we must use it constantly. The woman had no outstanding offenses, no record, and it wasn't a dangerous situation. Some people are going to be let off with a warning, or the cops will be writing tickets all day. Finding a balance between urgent and important is one way to keep the peace between police and civilians."

It occurred to me that every minute a police officer spends writing a ticket for something minor is time spent ignoring everything else.

I noticed throughout my ride-alongs that the officers on

patrol knew a lot of the individuals in the community by name and worked to develop relationships, even with people breaking the law and the people they'd arrested in the past.

I have a difficult time imagining trying to develop a friendly relationship with someone you know is doing wrong, probably lying to your face, and nonetheless doing what it takes to maintain some harmony between citizens and the police in the neighborhood. Not to arrest as many people as possible, not to give out a quota of tickets, but just maintain an equilibrium, a fragile peace, a managed chaos.

People in underprivileged neighborhoods have *nowhere to go*, so every business becomes a gathering place for the citizens. Barbershops and bodegas stay open until after midnight, just so ordinary folks can hang out.

When I was growing up in Brooklyn in the sixties and seventies, candy stores and newsstands stayed open on Saturday night, and the neighborhood men would sit around, order egg creams and milkshakes, and wait for the Sunday paper to arrive around midnight. It was a weekend ritual. There in the Bronx in 2023, it was every night in every possible place.

> People need a place to go; people want to gather.
> Individuals should be able to go to a park on a summer evening.

People need a place to go; people want to gather. Individuals should be able to go to a park on a summer evening. But the officers told me, "You can't go into any park—they're dangerous, they're drug-infested, nobody can just hang out in the park. So, we see people hanging out in front of their buildings, drinking, smoking hookahs, and playing music. Now come the three-one-one calls."

The service line 311 was created in cities to take the non-emergency pressure off the 911 lines. According to New York City, 311 "provides the public with quick, easy access to non-emergency government services and information." It's often used for complaints about noise, illegal parking, trash collection, or if you don't like your neighbor very much.

It can get loud out on the street, between boom boxes and cars with enormous blaring bass speakers and ordinary people noise. After the blacked-out windows incident, we patrolled and answered a 311 call. We pulled up to a group hanging out and blasting music. "Turn it down," the officers said, which the kids did, begrudgingly. As soon as we pulled away, the music turned back up. Now, we had to go back. No one claimed to be the owner of the boom box, so the cops confiscated it.

"Why'd they let you take their player?" I asked.

"Street economics," the officer replied. "Because the ticket costs more than another boom box."

To my surprise, the officers' phones blew up with these kinds of "quality of life" complaints. We spent the next two hours patrolling the neighborhood, trying to get people to turn the music down or off.

It was a night of constant confrontation. The cops attempted to mitigate noise without writing summonses, and the citizens were pissed off at the cops because they had no place to go for enjoyment.

In the Four-Six, and as I'd later notice in other precincts, I saw generational poverty, institutionalized racism, and boredom—all the things that contribute to a system that creates more kids, less education, and fewer opportunities for mentorship and guidance. And the police become scapegoats because they represent the system that seems to be breeding these issues. They are perceived as, literally, The Man.

CHAPTER 3

The Three-Two · *Manhattan*

*Words have energy and power with the
ability to help, to heal, to hinder, to hurt,
to harm, to humiliate, and to humble.*

—YEHUDA BERG, AMERICAN AUTHOR
AND FORMER TEACHER OF KABBALAH[2]

Manhattan isn't the Bronx. In some parts of Manhattan, you can move from upscale to underprivileged by crossing the street. The pace is slower in some neighborhoods. There are more places for recreation and entertainment.

My next ride-along was with the 32nd Precinct in East Harlem, the northeast corner of Manhattan. The precinct's jurisdiction includes six public housing complexes, eleven private housing developments, and the well-known Lenox Avenue business district from 132nd to 139th Streets.

The assignments in the Three-Two are more specialized than what I saw in the Bronx, with one team specifically looking for stolen cars, another looking for guns, and still another assigned to working with young people in the community.

I started riding with Officers Tyler Mason and Miguel

---

[2] Yehuda Berg, "The Power of Words," *Huffington Post*, September 14, 2010, https://www.huffpost.com/entry/the-power-of-words_b_716183.

Acevedo, who were assigned to GLA (Grand Larceny Auto). Riding with them, I learned some interesting things about police technology. To assist them in their search for stolen cars (an underground business that costs Americans up to $24 billion a year), the officers use a license plate reader, an onboard computer that checks license plates while the officers are cruising the area. Using this device, a police vehicle can enter a parking lot and check every license plate without stepping out of the car.

Officers Acevedo and Mason and me in front of the 32nd Precinct.

Looking at this precinct compared to the Four-Six in the Bronx, it seems that the 46th Precinct has a higher total number of complaints compared to the 32nd Precinct, but that varies by specific crimes. For example, there are more car thefts in East Harlem.

Frankly, I didn't think looking for stolen cars would be too exciting, but I was impressed with the officers' focus on the work they were doing. After a couple of hours, we took some 311 calls, which were a shortcut to getting a feel for the neighborhood and the issues concerning its citizens, mostly apartment dwellers with noise complaints.

I found the idea of "specializing" compelling, and beyond stolen cars, there are so many other areas in which the officers at the Three-Two are dedicated. Erika Gonzalez, an officer with the Three-Two since 2019, is focused on the youth in the community. She follows up on kids who have been in trouble, visits the Boys & Girls Club of East Harlem to work with young people, and she's an example of what the NYPD is trying to do to manage the up-and-comers, to keep them out of trouble or at least out of more significant trouble. That shows the NYPD's commitment to preventing crime by playing the long game—if you can keep young kids from getting into bad situations, you might keep them from turning to crime.

If you can keep young kids from getting into bad situations, you might keep them from turning to crime.

Later, I got to ride with Lieutenant Jose Ramos and Officer Jose Tavarez. Officer Tavarez has been a cop since 2010 and at the Three-Two since 2021. Lieutenant Ramos has been in the NYPD since 2008.

These guys weren't answering calls—they were looking for people who were looking for trouble. Their job was to find individuals who were on the edge of crime and negotiate them away from it.

We noticed a man barbecuing and selling chicken on the sidewalk. Permit? No. Ramos and Tavarez told the man to pack it up.

"Oh, don't worry," the guy said, "this is the last of it. I'm just finishing this one chicken, then I'm done."

While the chicken chef showed them an empty box, the officers observed another big cooler off to the side. One officer took the container and gently told the man, "Look, we both know you're not finishing. You just put brand-new coals on that fire."

In both East Harlem and the Bronx, many people on the street seem to view the police as an occupying force: us versus them.

I noticed the tone of the officer was calm and respectful. Ramos and Tavarez were communicating using Verbal Judo. The art of Judo involves using an opponent's energy to deflect and overcome. Verbal Judo is a technique for redirecting behavior with words, created by George J. Thompson, PhD, to educate individuals in de-escalation. The officers I rode with were very good at it. They approached citizens who were doing wrong and held them accountable to the truth, but they did so with empathy and respect. It sounds easier than it is, but in a potentially volatile situation (like when talking to a guy with a barbecue full of hot coals), it's a crucial skill.

The use of Verbal Judo engages people instead of confronting them by having an ordinary conversation and not an interrogation. Then, the officers watch to see how people react or respond. Will they get nervous? Will they scamper, or are they just hanging out?

In both East Harlem and the Bronx, many people on the street seem to view the police as an occupying force: *us versus them*. The police get cursed out a lot. The officers I was with had a thin line to walk—not to be too aggressive but still present themselves with authority. It's like the balance and harmony the officers in the Bronx spoke about. And if someone is breaking the law, then decisions must be made.

For instance, I saw several examples of public defecation. Sure, you might see a guy urinating between cars, but this was a woman in the middle of the street, unclothed and squatting.

"What you looking at?!" she shouted.

Were these officers going to give her a summons?

"We could," they answered, "but the paperwork isn't worth it."

Then, there was a car stopped at the corner, and the driver was talking with people standing on the corner. We saw some sort of exchange where they tried to make it look like they were shaking hands while passing a small object. It was an unmistakable drug deal, although we couldn't see what drug was being dealt.

We pulled up, and the individuals scattered, so Officer Tavarez approached the driver. It turned out the driver was on parole. He let the cops search his vehicle, in which there was a knapsack full of weed on the seat. So now what? It's a minor crime, selling marijuana without a license. The officers could've called it in, but the only result would be the man's parole revocation. Who does that help? So they let him go.

Then we saw a man about sixty-five years old, smoking crack in front of a building. The officers had to approach, because crack isn't weed, but they didn't want to put him in jail. While speaking to the man calmly and respectfully, the officers retrieved his drugs. Still, the officers explained they knew he'd have to figure out how to get more, indicating a frustrating cycle.

Throughout the evening, Ramos and Tavarez pulled up to random citizens hanging out on the street and started seemingly innocuous conversations using Verbal Judo: "What's up? How you doing?"

"Huh? Why you talking to me? What do you want?" were many of the responses.

"I'm just the neighborhood cop," Ramos said. "Can't we just have a conversation?"

Meanwhile, Tavarez was taking everything in, observing the guy, the street, and whatever was going on in fine detail, so when we came around the block again in two to five minutes, they'd know if anything had changed, if anything suspicious was going on.

It occurred to me that this tactic of scanning and detailed observation would also work in most management situations. Many managers have implemented the "Management by Wandering Around (MBWA)" idea, moving around the office and having little chats with employees, but this idea of moving more slowly and taking everything in, really noticing and engaging, and encouraging others to talk would make MBWA work much more effectively.

On the street, the conversations were designed to engage but even more to detect. One of the cops' missions is to get guns off the street. Unfortunately, they can't see what's in the pockets of the people they're engaging, so they look for subtle details, for "tells." In most cases, the only tell is kids telling the cops to go fuck themselves. Again, there is an astonishing amount of verbal abuse against the people who are supposed to be there to serve and protect. I learned later from speaking with community leaders that despite the officers' best efforts, many citizens still don't feel served, they don't feel protected, even though the statistics show a reduction in crime.

> Despite the officers' best efforts, many citizens still don't feel served, they don't feel protected.

At the same time, what I saw was, again, citizens with nowhere to go and wanting more police presence but not interference. Kids and adults can't go into the little pocket parks after dark, so why not make the public spaces safer? Why can't the precinct have a couple of officers on foot in the park so people can have a place to hang out, say, until 10 p.m.?

But what do I know?

I had more to learn.

CHAPTER 4

Community Leader Russell Smith · *Harlem*

The police are the public and the public are the police.
—Sir Robert Peel, "Father of Modern Policing"

One big hole in my knowledge was the community perspective. What did people who live in the city think of the cops? What ideas did citizens have for improving the current situation? Were there individuals who were organizing the community and engaging with the police, and if so, who were they?

I did what I do: I asked around and began networking. Someone suggested that I speak to "Big Russ" Smith in Harlem.

A thoughtful, energetic man with an infectious smile, Russell Smith is a driving force in the Harlem community. In addition to serving as president of the Community Council for the 32nd Precinct, Smith is an entrepreneur and a master barber whose Big Russ Barber Training Program helps at-risk youth get off the street and into a trade.

He's a well-known community activist who has his finger on the pulse of the sentiments of his neighbors, who say they believe the police are not on their side. Russ is well aware of the history of his community and the confrontational relationship that has long existed between his fellow citizens and the police, a gap I would see throughout other ride-alongs inside and outside the city. I was glad to learn he would make the time to speak with me. We met on Zoom—me from my office and Russ from his front porch.

Big Russ Smith stands in front of his barber shop in Harlem.

I asked Russ about his perspective on why people in the community might have a negative view of the police and what he thought it would take to improve the relationship between the community and the cops.

"It varies," Russ said, the sun shining on one side of his face on a warm August afternoon. "How police officers relate to the community depends on the laws and the officers' training. Once they're trained, they need a commanding officer of the precinct who ensures that field training, training on the street, is handled in a certain way. You don't always get that, so at times, situations get out of hand. When conflicts get out of hand, confrontations start building up, and you have an uproar. So, now, who has to come in and bridge that gap of resentment between the cops and the citizens? The advocates of the community, the people who have the voices.

"And there are only a certain number of voices that matter across this city," Russ continued. "Out of, say, thirty community voices, you might have three people that really matter, that the police department will respect and sit down with. And then it comes down to politics."

I asked Russ if he was talking about himself.

"I've been president of the Thirty-Second Precinct Council for a long time. I've seen it all. One thing I don't get caught up in . . . I don't do the politics thing," Russ said, leaning back in his chair. "If I see that you're an amazing cop, that you've been treating the community well, then I'm going to call the commander and say, 'Hey, this guy's great, you should do something with him, et cetera.'

"And the people downtown at One Police Plaza call me," he chuckled, "like I'm the boss: 'How's such and such doing?' and I might say, 'His door is always closed. He's not receptive. You guys have to get someone up here who wants to deal with the community.'"

I wanted Russ to get specific about the way the community's relationship with the police has changed and how it has remained the same. "Tell me about the community," I asked.

"You have to know the history of the precinct," Russ told me. "No matter how much wealth Harlem gets, there are always going to be killings and shootings. People don't know that in the Thirty-second Precinct, there are two blocks that have been in a rivalry for over fifty years. *Over fifty years.* That's not going to stop; it goes on to this day. That's a heads-up I will give to every commanding officer that comes to this precinct. Over five decades of rivalry—nephews, cousins—it's different from other neighborhoods. And if you get a cop who thinks he's tough by being disrespectful, the whole precinct is going to have problems."

I knew he meant that disrespect breeds disrespect, and the kind of friction that produces more heat than light.

"It's a tough command, the Three-Two," Russ said.

"Do you only meet with the commanders, or do you speak to the rank and file?" I asked.

"I go to speak to the new officers at roll call," Russ answered. "And what I tell the new officers is: 'I understand your training. What they taught you in the Academy is great, but being out here on the streets is a different beast. You got to have street smarts and work smarts. They didn't teach you the streets at the Academy.' The other thing I always tell them: The number-one thing that people hate in these communities is to be talked down to."

I pointed out that he was talking about emotional intelligence, empathy, and common sense, which a young officer can learn from watching an older officer.

Russ nodded and added, "The issue that escalates things is how officers talk to people. Even me, with my experience, credentials, and relationships with the police, if I get pulled over tomorrow and you talk down to me, if you're disrespectful and rude, as a man, I can't allow you to talk to me like that. My reaction depends on the words coming out of your mouth. We could get into a shouting match. As a human being, it's a respect thing. If I allow it, you're going to do it with every person you pull over!"

I wanted Russ to address the tension between police and young people, and I talked about the specialized focus of Officer Erika Gonzalez on youth. "Do you think the cops should get involved with the schools and develop rapport with the neighborhood kids, or is that just wishful thinking?"

"The police should do more," Russ said. "That way, they would get to know the local culture and get to know what's going on. They would learn what ticks kids off."

"Is any of this outreach going on today? Is it getting better?"

Russ said, "You know, I have to commend the NYPD in the current administration for what Mayor Eric Adams is doing, along with Mark Stewart [Deputy Commissioner of Community Affairs] I haven't seen this much engagement in the community with the police department in years."

"I haven't seen this much engagement in the community with the police department in years."

"Like what?"

"For one thing, baby showers," he said. "This has never happened before."

I had to look this up myself—since 2022, the NYPD has been hosting community baby showers for hundreds of moms-to-be, where corporate-donated items like diapers, formula, toys, etc., are given to expecting mothers by the NYPD Community Affairs Bureau. This isn't paid for by tax dollars. Businesses provide the gifts; the NYPD distributes them.

"Do you know how different that is, in these communities, with expectant parents who don't have money for strollers, Pampers—that is *big*. That is huge. The city is holding baby showers! I've been going to baby showers my whole life, where people just wish someone would bring formula. I've got seven kids; I know what it is to have nothing and now to have diapers, milk, and toys.

"And also," Russ added, "at Christmas, they're giving out tons of toys! It goes with the administration, with what

[Mayor] Eric Adams is doing. Whatever people say about him, let's see what he's doing. He's trying to create jobs. He's doing the baby showers; he's involved in the communities."

Russ continued, "Mayor Adams just hired a guy, Keith Howard, as Commissioner of the Department of Youth and Community Development. These guys are amazing and stay under the radar. That department funds peer violence initiatives, all the after-school and summer school programs, and they create more programs for kids. They've asked me to create and instruct a six-week pilot filmmaking program to teach kids the craft. They're going the extra step, and most people don't know about it.

"City Hall and the NYPD are connected with helping get kids off the street, bridging the gap, and pointing them in the right direction. In my barber training program, I get to work with youth offenders, kids coming out of the Children's Services system, out of treatment centers, and we're getting them a trade. We've got fifteen graduates this year with apprentice licenses. Some of these guys have felony convictions. Who's helping them? It was my dream to open a barber school. Now, I have the first Black-owned barber training program in New York City. This is what I do. The Three-Two is right across the street, and I always invite the cops to come across the street to get a haircut. Then I invite them to come and speak to the class. We've had an ex-commissioner and the chief of department join us."

I wasn't familiar with the term "chief of department." That role is the highest-ranking uniformed officer in the NYPD, reporting directly to the commissioner.

"I see what's going on and what's needed in the community," Russ said. "I met my wife at the Thirty-Second Precinct; we've been married for eleven years, together for thirteen."

"Wait," I said, "your wife is a police officer?"

"Yes. My wife is a detective."

I had one more question. "Are there opportunities for a

person in the community to talk to the police, or is that kind of communication something that still needs to be improved?"

"Once again," Russ said, "it's the precinct's commanding officer who sets the tone, whose door should always be open. One example: when Inspector [Amir] Yakatally, an amazing guy, left as commanding officer of the Three-Two, I sat down with the new C.O., Bryan Natale, to explain what this community is about. He listened. He came to council meetings. He told me he would be putting officers back on the beat. He said, 'I want my officers interacting with the community. I'm giving them flyers to hand out, inviting people to community meetings.' He's been consistent with that from day one. When you have leadership like that, someone who's trying to bridge the gap, that's a start. That's all I ask for: to show interest in the community and keep the relationships going."

"People respond to fairness, being straight on point, and leaving the politics on the side."

Russ is a leader who not only has identified problems but has ideas for solutions, ending our video chat by saying, "The best approach is for the cops to get out more. Call these big town hall meetings with the officers and the bosses in one spot. Roll out a yearly plan and put it into the community—make it a two-way street where everyone holds each other accountable. You respect us, and we respect you. If an officer disrespects a citizen, let the cops know, and at the same time, citizens can't disrespect the officers. You get a better response if you roll out a program like that. People respond to fairness, being straight on point, and leaving the politics on the side."

CHAPTER 5

The Seven-Three · *Brooklyn*

*Brooklyn is not the easiest place to grow up in,
although I wouldn't change that experience for anything.*

—Singer-songwriter Neil Diamond

New York City consists of five boroughs: Manhattan, the Bronx, Brooklyn, Queens, and Staten Island. In a ride-along with officers of the 73rd Precinct in Ocean Hill/Brownsville, Brooklyn, I'd cover my third borough and fourth precinct. Summer was coming to a close quickly, and I'd spend this shift seeing a very different Brooklyn than the one I had been raised in.

Ocean Hill/Brownsville are two neighborhoods in one precinct, with about 100,000 people living there. Although I was born in what is now Brookdale University Hospital and Medical Center, almost exactly one mile from the Seven-Three station house, I don't remember ever being in either neighborhood before. My brother Cary claims to have had his first slice of pizza in Brownsville, but that was before I was born.

The precinct headquarters is on New York Avenue. Around the corner on Bristol Street, 400 feet away, is the Crossroads Juvenile Center, which I first mistook for the police station. It was an easy error—the place looks like a jail, almost a block long with a lot of barbed wire.

Someone directed me around the corner to the precinct.

The place was buzzing. I had just missed a local shooting less than half an hour before I arrived. Even where I stood, just inside the front doors, I could hear the shouting and banging and carrying on from the cells.

The 73rd Precinct has long been considered the most dangerous precinct in Brooklyn, with Brownsville once called the "murder capital of New York." Even though violent crime and murder are way down, I don't think anyone would describe it as a safe place.

Like every other precinct I visited, their rosters are down between 20 and 25 percent since 2022.

And like every other precinct I visited, their rosters are down between 20 and 25 percent since 2022. Some of that is because of city-wide budget cuts, but I keep hearing how hard it is to attract and retain good cops.

As with every other ride-along, we did the evening shift, 4 p.m. to midnight. What I saw a lot of were homeless shelters and gangs. I also saw some very nice-looking parks that citizens were afraid to enter.

We drove by the Plaza Residences, an apartment complex that looked pretty okay in the daylight. However, there were a lot of young men wearing red, which the officers informed me signified their allegiance to the Bloods gang whose territory included the Plaza. This area, they told me, was a hotbed of gang activity.

We drove past what I thought was a liquor store with one young man standing outside, but I learned it wasn't what it seemed.

"That guy is the lookout," one of the officers said. "See the one wearing the red hoodie?"

I nodded. "So, they're selling more than booze in there?" I asked.

"Yeah, they deal drugs in there."

"And you can't do anything?"

"Not in that hole, no. As soon as we walk in, the guy at the counter starts making noises, so they all stop what they're doing."

Without probable cause or witnessing something, the police can't intervene.

"Okay," I said. "What about that park—is it safe?" I asked, already knowing the answer.

"I wouldn't say *safe*," the officer chuckled. "We try to do hourly *directeds*, where we park the car facing the park and turn the lights on to try and help the people in the neighborhood feel safer."

"What does *directed* mean in police jargon?" I asked.

"Technically, *directed* refers to special attention to a specific area due to a current condition. And there," the officer said as we turned onto Sutter Avenue, "is the Langston Hughes Projects. One of our worst developments."

Langston Hughes Houses, as the Seven-Three in general, is plagued by gun violence, perpetrated mainly by rival gangs and their subsets. The gang known as WOOO is based in the Langston Hughes Houses. Their main rival is a gang called CHOO. The two gangs have been at war with each other since 2010. The age of these gang members ranges from seventeen to twenty-seven, and their numbers are difficult to gauge. What's not hard to gauge is the violence of the two gangs. When they have a shootout, the officers told me, bystanders are not a consideration.

I don't know much about literature, but I know Langston

Hughes was a great American poet and social activist. He innovated the art form known as jazz poetry and was a leader in the Harlem Renaissance. It is a shame that a place named for him has come to be better known for brutality and bloodshed.

The Seven-Three covers eighteen housing projects, more than any other area of the city, with about 10,000 units inside 100 buildings within one square mile, according to NYC.gov. To say the least, it's crowded and unsafe. The NYPD has a dedicated housing bureau, but it looks like WOOO, the Bloods' affiliate gang, runs the Hughes Houses. There were *a lot* of young men wearing red.

Every 911 call we took that evening was a domestic disturbance. In fact, I've learned that there are nearly 600 calls of domestic violence across the city every day. I saw partners threatening each other, committing violence against each other, and ultimately calling the cops on each other. It was difficult and distressing to see how many people live afraid, and even more heart-wrenching to see individuals scared of the people in their own homes.

I thought about how some people don't get to feel safe in their own homes living with people that were supposed to be their loved ones.

The last call I went along on that evening was to visit a woman who had called 911 because she said she was afraid that her husband was going to shoot her. Our visit turned into an hour-long debacle with the two officers trying to get the husband to leave the apartment, convincing him that he wasn't going to jail (they wanted to take him to the hospital for a psychiatric evaluation), the woman in tears, and both of them terrified of whatever was to come next. The officers were kind and empathetic, using a subtle form of Verbal Judo to deescalate the situation.

Eventually, one of the backup vehicles took the husband to the hospital, and we moved on.

I wondered how the story ended, but we weren't given that kind of detail. Most uniformed cops get used to doing the job without the resolution of learning the outcome. What happened to the husband? The wife? We didn't know. I thought about how some people don't get to feel safe in their own homes, living with people who were supposed to be their loved ones. My tension was mingled with sadness.

I was on edge through the entire ride. While my time in the Seven-Three didn't have the level of intensity I'd experienced in the Bronx, there was this constant undertone of danger that kept my adrenaline pumping. I had had enough well before the shift ended, and I was ready to go home and feel safe.

CHAPTER 6

The Seven-Seven · *Crown Heights, Brooklyn*

People from Brooklyn grow up with a certain common sense. If it doesn't ring true, it's not true.

—Judge Judy Sheindlin ("Judge Judy")[3]

The 77th Precinct is adjacent to the 73rd and covers the northern portion of the Crown Heights section of Brooklyn and part of Prospect Heights. It's a wide, narrow area, 1.2 square miles, and shaped almost like a box of saltine crackers on the map, stretching from Grand Army Plaza on its western border to Brownsville on the eastern. This neighborhood has been gentrifying, with older buildings being renovated and sold to people with money, so there's a mix of poverty and middle-class life along with expanding pockets of wealth.

This precinct also suffered from a significant decline in the number of officers and staff. The Seven-Seven has about 130 officers, down from approximately 200 since 2022. All over the city, the problem was the same—the old guard was retiring, and recruiting new officers was a challenge.

---

3 CNN Transcripts, "CNN Larry King Live: Interview with Judge Judy," aired November 10, 2010, https://transcripts.cnn.com/show/lkl/date/2010-11-10/segment/01.

The precinct has seventeen detectives, also a steep decline. As one of the detectives described his job to me, he told me something that shocked me. He said that he was one of two detectives in the precinct who each handled *three hundred domestic violence cases a year*, and each one had to be investigated.

If you figure a five-day workweek, there are about 250 working days in a year, so these detectives have more than one domestic violence call a day that they have to investigate. Maybe the problem is more social than legal. Maybe people need some help living together.

When it was time to ride, I joined Officers Brian Kalt and Abdul Ahmad, both experienced officers, having served for more than five years each. While we rode on this relatively quiet four-to-midnight shift, I asked them about the neighborhood and what they had to deal with. I began with "How much of the precinct do you cover?"

"About a fourth," Officer Kalt said.

"Do you have issues with gangs?" I asked next.

"There's some gang activity," Kalt replied. "They're mostly sects, sub-gangs of the Bloods, like WOOO and CHOO, and they beef with each other."

To try to compare with the Seven-Three next door, I asked, "So, how many of these sects are in this small area?"

"We've got about five active right now, "Officer Ahmad answered. "It changes; it fluctuates. Some guys get locked up. A few get out of the life."

I was surprised at the difference between the look of this precinct and that of the precinct next door. The Seven-Three had a lot of housing projects and homeless shelters. I wasn't seeing as much of either in the Seven-Seven. The parks looked safer and more welcoming without the air of menace at the entrance.

"We're a little luckier than the Seven-Three," Officer Ahmad said. "It's not go-go-go all the time."

"Sometimes it's real busy; other times there's nothing going on," agreed Officer Kalt.

This wasn't a busy night, but I saw another part of Brooklyn I didn't know growing up. After all, I only lived in Crown Heights until I was two years old, which was long ago.

We drove by the historic Weeksville area, which I'd never seen or even heard of. Weeksville was one of the first areas in New York City where African-Americans could own homes. Four historic landmark homes, known as the Hunterfly Road Houses, serve as a museum: the Weeksville Heritage Center.

I don't know how they do it. In the precincts I've visited and the ride-alongs I've done, one thing I did not see was cops sitting around eating doughnuts.

In another section, the officers showed me examples of mixed-use buildings comprising 25 percent low-income affordable apartments and 75 percent "supportive housing" for the mentally ill. Ahmad pointed out one of the flaws in this system: "People who aren't suffering from anything are being harassed by those who are ill, and sometimes that sparks violence."

Every ride-along so far—the Bronx, Manhattan, and Brooklyn—showed me pain, fear, violence, drugs, poverty, citizens buried under challenging circumstances, and a police force that could do little more than shovel sand against the tide to maintain an unacceptable status quo.

Riding along with the cops was starting to get to me. I found myself looking over my shoulder, experiencing jumpiness, and overreacting to noises even in my everyday life. I don't know how they do it. In the precincts I've visited and the ride-alongs I've done, one thing I did not see was cops sitting around eating doughnuts. I don't know where that stereotype comes from, but the officers I met are hardworking public servants; they barely had time to eat dinner. I'm sure there are bad cops in New York City, just like there are bad people everywhere, but it's a hard job, and the people I met were doing the challenging work and doing it as best they could.

I'd only been on a few ride-alongs, but I was burning out. I was sad, nervous, exhausted, and surprisingly easily scared. It seemed like nobody had any idea how to fix anything, despite what I'd learned from Big Russ Smith. My two fundamental leadership principles have always been: Fix what's broken, and improve on what's already working. I was looking at a situation where nobody seemed to know how to fix what was broken. And was any policy going well enough to make it even better? Was gentrification creating less crime, or was it making the older residents more hostile? I needed to speak to another civilian in the community to learn more.

CHAPTER 7

Community Leader Lisa Kenner • *Brownsville*

*We cannot always build the future for our youth,
but we can build our youth for the future.*

—Franklin D. Roosevelt[4]

Lisa Kenner was born and raised in the Van Dyke Houses in Brownsville, Brooklyn. Van Dyke is a large housing project, and Brownsville is a densely populated part of Brooklyn, with about 130,000 residents in just over one square mile. Ms. Kenner, a short-haired woman with a ready smile and an unmistakable Brooklyn accent, has been president of the Van Dyke Houses Resident Association for the past twenty years, bringing her considerable energies to the project and doing all she can to make and keep Van Dyke Houses a place where people can feel safe and happy raising families.

In her lifetime of experience at Van Dyke, Lisa Kenner has worked with and dealt with the NYPD and the NYC Housing

---

4 Gerhard Peters and John T. Woolley, "Franklin D. Roosevelt, Address at the University of Pennsylvania, September 20, 1940," The American Presidency Project, https://www.presidency.ucsb.edu/documents/address-university-pennsylvania.

Police (which is now part of the NYPD), and she graciously met with me on Zoom to share her experiences and ideas.

"I've never had an incident with the police," Ms. Kenner told me. "But one time, a police officer said something out of the way, and I had to correct him. He was a white officer, and he made a statement in front of some of our seniors that women in Brownsville had babies by different men. Everybody just looked at him because there were some older women who had had children, and he didn't even know he was being rude.

Lisa Kenner [third from left] at a local community event.

"So, I said, 'Why would you say that? Did your mother tell you something like that? We've got good women in Brownsville.' I called him Dennis the Menace. He would have to get away from here because if he felt like that about women, whether he's Black or white, he didn't need to be in Van Dyke."

"Would you say that's a general attitude, or was that a one-time thing?" I asked.

"That was the first time I ever heard that. Then I took it to the captain, who asked me, 'Ms. Kenner, have you ever said something you shouldn't have said?' and I said, 'Yeah, but I ain't a police officer.' Everybody says things they shouldn't, but it's different when you're in a position of authority. And I said that officer shouldn't stay here if that's how he thinks about Black women. Most of the people who live here are women, and many of them are single. Then I found out the officer didn't really know any Black people. When a white officer who doesn't socialize with Black people, who didn't go to school with Black people, comes into this area, he has to be brought in, mentored by an officer who knows the community, or there's going to be some culture shock."

So, new officers should be mentored or "brought in" to get to know the community, which mirrored something Big Russ had said about training on the street: "I want … officers interacting with the community."

"What were some positive interactions with the police?" I asked. I wanted to know the flipside of her experience, too.

"I used to like the J-RIP [Juvenile Robbery Intervention Program]. These kids had gotten in trouble, but the police officers used to work with them. If they had to go to job training or something, they'd drop them off and make sure they go check in. The officers would check on them at home, too. At Christmastime, the families of those kids would get together with the police officers. And one of the best basketball games I've ever seen was those young people playing against the police."

This made me curious. "How did that come about?" I asked.

"My basketball team," she said. "We had guys from different housing developments get together. People said, 'You can't go across that street,' but that wasn't so. We had players from rival buildings. Tilden, Van Dyke, Unity, Langston Hughes, Seth Low, Howard—they all came together and played ball with the police. Those were good games, but the main thing was that the police got to know who these kids were. That led to one of the officers coming to me and saying, 'I've seen one of your boys with a certain group of people, and that's not good.' He didn't want to approach the kid—he wanted me to approach him. These kids don't think anybody's watching. I tell them somebody's always watching."

I pictured those basketball games and how unifying they must have been. I felt disappointed that they hadn't continued. "What happened with that program?" I asked.

"The city has pulled police out of the neighborhood and put them on the trains. We don't see them as much. You've got to police yourself."

I thought about what Russ Smith had said, how it all comes down to the precinct commander. Harlem was increasing the police presence, and according to Ms. Kenner, Brownsville was not.

"You don't have cops on the beat here?" I asked.

"We're getting some out here now, but it's not the same as when I grew up in Van Dyke. I've been here sixty-five years, and I remember when you couldn't walk on the grass without getting a ten-dollar fine. It's all different now."

"In what other ways is it different?"

"The police don't really greet you. They don't initiate. If I walk past and say, 'Good afternoon,' *then* they'll say 'good afternoon.' There was a time when new officers came in, they walked them through the streets, and if they saw me, they'd say, 'Ms. Kenner, this is officer such-and-such,' you'd get to see them, and they'd get to see you, you know? But they haven't been doing that. They should. If you're going to work in the community, the community needs to see you, and you need to see them. Then, God forbid, if something happens, you have a relationship instead of coming in unknown and getting people's backs up. You've got to get to know them. Detective

Brant [Walter J. Brant, NYPD] used to bring the new recruits to meet us, but I think he's getting ready to retire. He's been here like thirty years. Everybody knows Brant. He may be a white police officer, but everybody knows him."

"If you're going to work in the community, the community needs to see you, and you need to see them."

The way Ms. Kenner described it, as the new generation of police were being assigned to the precinct, relationships were not being forged between them and the community. I asked, "Is there a gap, with older police officers who know the community retiring?" I asked. "Is it more difficult being policed by younger cops?"

"Yes, the force is younger now, and they need to be brought into the community. Here in Police Service Area Two, which serves the NYC Housing Authority developments in three separate precincts, we have regular meetings. Captain Sean Claxton, the commander, brings in the officers, so you get to know the officers, and they get to know you."

"How often is that?"

"We have that once a month," Ms. Kenner continued. "It's nice to have that. One time, I went to the store at about eleven o'clock at night, and the police were out there. One said, 'Ms. Kenner, what are you doing outside?' That was a good feeling.

"But something's happening since the pandemic. I don't understand it; it's so different. Everybody's on edge. I see young men sitting on a bench, and they're leery of the police. I mean, I'd rather see them sitting than running around getting in trouble, but they don't interact with the police, and the police don't interact with them. It's tense.

"Look, I'm not a man, but I can see how it's different to be a Black man in the neighborhood and feel like the police are always looking at you. I've seen it for myself: young men walking down the street, and all of a sudden, the police just stop them. You can't walk down the street with more than two men—you'll be stopped. Even just going to play basketball or something. But it's not the same for women, and women can be just as deadly as men, but the cops aren't going to bother them." That mirrored some of what I'd seen on the street. Bias or some kind of misplaced chivalry?

"What do you think needs to happen," I asked, "to improve the relationship between police and community? What would you want to put in play? Is there a way to make the police part of the scene instead of just standing there or picking on groups of young men?"

"I'll tell you, the PSA2 commander, Captain Sean Claxton started a meeting where each person would bring five young men to the meeting. Well, that's how it started off, but some people didn't want to come across the street! Other developments like Tilden didn't want to come to Van Dyke, Van Dyke didn't want to go to Tilden. So what happened? We have a flag football team and some cheerleaders, and it's not just Van Dyke. We've got kids from Tilden. I do an empowerment workshop for the kids at least once a month, so the first person to come in is the captain to talk to the kids. Some of these kids are only seven years old, but you've got to get them young; you can't wait until they're fourteen or fifteen. So that was a break, an opportunity. When they see him in the street, they can say, 'Hey, Captain, remember me from the community center?' It's a start.

"But out on the street, it's different. I remember when Chief Maddrey [former Chief of Department Jeffrey Maddrey] was commanding officer at the Seventy-Third Precinct; that was the first time I had ever seen a captain bring his family to National Night Out."

National Night Out, a forty-year-old nationwide program designed to bring police and communities together in a positive environment, is a great bridge-builder. Cops and citizens come together for an evening of planned festivities and getting to know one another.

"It meant something that he brought his wife and children to a community event," Ms. Kenner added. I nodded.

"Ms. Kenner, if I put you in front of all the cadets at the Police Academy and you had them for fifteen minutes, what are the two things you want to tell those police officers knowing what you know? What would you want to insert in their minds before they ever walk out to the street?"

"I would tell them that if you want respect, you've got to give respect. I would tell them the same thing I tell my grandchildren. Be respectful. It's hard to trust, so you have to earn trust." Ms. Kenner went on, "In a job like the police, you have to be on point; if you're not, maybe that's not the job for you. Not everybody is a criminal. At the same time, I would tell them that they have to watch their backs. At the end of the day, everybody, police or not, wants to get home safe."

National Night Out, a forty-year-old nationwide program designed to bring police and communities together in a positive environment, is a great bridge-builder.

"One thing the police did that I liked was we got to pick our own captain! We got to interview them and ask questions of the two candidates [they had] for captain, and we picked a good one. And the fact that we had that opportunity showed caring and respect for the community."

It's apparent Lisa Kenner values respect and communication. She holds certain police in high regard, and she respects the job they do.

"I'm glad God didn't call me to be police," she said.

It's also clear that both she and Big Russ Smith (and probably most community members) find disrespect and being talked down to are the most consistent problems in the communities. They'd like to see more respect on both sides.

CHAPTER 8

A Small City Comparison · *Syracuse, New York*

Anyone who thinks small towns are friendlier than big cities lives in a big city.

—Richard Peck, American novelist[5]

The next step in my journey was to find out if policing elsewhere is like policing in New York City, with its precinct divisions, distinct neighborhoods, and constant tensions. I wanted to make a comparison with a smaller city. Do they patrol the same way? Are there inner-city neighborhoods? Does that make policing more difficult? I knew just the place.

I'd spent four years of my life in a small city in Upstate New York when I attended Syracuse University. My blood runs Orange, Syracuse University's official color since 1890. I was going to Syracuse.

About a four-hour drive from New York City, Syracuse is the fifth most-populated city in New York State with 146,000 residents and covers about twenty-five-and-a-half square miles. It has a couple of lakes, a sizeable creek, an international

---
5 Richard Peck, *A Year Down Yonder* (Penguin Young Readers Group, 2002), 28.

airport, and twenty-six separate and distinct neighborhoods. I know Syracuse well.

As an alumnus of the university, I've tried to do my part for the university and the city, but I had never closely observed the challenges the community and the Syracuse Police Department might have. So I arranged a ride-along on a Saturday, on the 4 p.m. to midnight shift, and scheduled a breakfast meeting the following morning with Mark Rusin, the Deputy Chief of Police in command of the Uniform Bureau. In addition to patrol officers, the Uniform Bureau includes Animal Cruelty and Dog Control, the School Information and Resource Program (SIRP), and Traffic Control.

One patrol car can be called to any part of the city
and has a lot of technology to assist.

Deputy Chief Rusin has been with the department since 2006. He built a reputation with his work on the implementation of the department's body-worn camera program, updated department policies and procedures, and police reform initiatives. A slim, bespectacled man with close-cropped hair graying at the temples, Rusin has quite a résumé. He has served as a uniformed officer, a detective, an instructor, and a community liaison. I knew he'd be the guy with the answers to any questions I might have after my ride-along.

I was assigned to ride with Officers Richard Solomon and Evan Francisco. The car was a Ford Explorer, and like most police cars, it was black and white and clean, inside and out. That night, there were only twenty-five officers on duty in the entire city (the Syracuse Police Department has about 400 officers in total).

Notably, Syracuse has a robust Division 1 sports program, drawing upwards of 150,000 people into the city at any given time. On the night of my ride-along, the Syracuse football team had just lost 31 to 14 to Clemson.

Since there was a big game at the JMA Wireless Dome on campus, I knew most of the police presence would be transferred from patrolling the streets to inside the dome, because that's where alcohol-related aggression and fighting generally occur. I'd seen fans carried out on stretchers. Fortunately, there were a lot of cops in attendance at the game to serve and protect the 40,973 spectators.

I learned the next day from the deputy chief that university sports, especially football and basketball, are a significant drain on police department resources, especially big games when additional cops get ordered in on a Saturday to police a game.

* * *

The police force in Syracuse is more centralized than the NYPD. It's not broken down into precincts. Cops from the North Side will zip down to the South Side when needed, and the South Side is where most of the crime is. According to Officer Francisco, gangs, shootings, and homicides are virtually all on Syracuse's South Side. The University is east of the center of the city, midway between North and South. We were patrolling the North side of town.

"The North Side is all over the board," Officer Solomon told me. "We could have a domestic that turns into a stolen vehicle, then suddenly, it's a rape, and we're like, 'WHOA! What is going on here?' It *looks* less dangerous on the North Side, with newer housing, but it's just a different atmosphere than the South Side."

> The pace moved slower in Syracuse; crime was hourly instead of minute by minute.

The largest shopping mall in New York State is Destiny USA, located on the West Side of Syracuse between North and South. It's six stories tall, with a basement floor. Destiny has movie theaters, restaurants, 250 stores, and, from the rumors I hear, rampant crime. As we patrolled, I asked the officers about the rumors. Unfortunately (or maybe fortunately), we didn't get to visit the mall itself.

"In any big area that's accessible to the public, where you have varying socioeconomic statuses and a lot of business, there's going to be crime there," Officer Solomon explained while we drove around Syracuse.

That was a political answer, but it suggested to me that the rumors were true.

The pace moved slower in Syracuse; crime was hourly instead of minute by minute. At about midnight, we got a call about a potential breaking and entering.

We pulled up in front of the house and Solomon and Francisco stepped out. As I'd been taught, I stayed a foot behind them. A drunk woman was trying to break into her brother's house.

The officers told her, "Get in an Uber and go home or go to jail."

"I'm staying here," the woman said.

The officers went back and forth with her, giving her the same two choices: Uber or jail. Eventually, they called a second car, which took her to jail.

Now, I don't know anything about policing, but I do know how to close a deal. I told the officers what I knew: "You weren't giving that woman the right choices. She's drunk; she's not thinking clearly."

I'll give these cops credit; they were attentive and focused on what I was saying. I went on, "You were empathetic. You were reasoning with her. But when someone's impaired, you can't reason with them; there's no reasoning available. You have to take control without telling them what to do. Give them multiple choices where every outcome is a good one. For example, 'Is there someone else you can stay with, or would you rather go home?'"

One thing I noticed riding along with cops in Syracuse was that there's just as much dysfunction there as there is in the Bronx—it's just more spread out. People aren't piled on top of one another, and there are a lot more trees. Instead of recognizing poverty by skyscraping housing projects, I saw it in ramshackle houses with paper-thin walls and broken windows. And the same kind of crime and mental health issues, the same drugs and drunkenness, were all just as present.

Breakfast with the Deputy Chief

The following day, I met with Deputy Chief Mark Rusin for breakfast and asked him my primary question: "What's the number-one problem you're facing right now that can potentially be solved?"

His answer didn't surprise me. "Staffing is the biggest problem," he replied. "Not just in Syracuse, but everywhere."

I knew he was right because I heard this everywhere I went. "Is it a recruiting problem or a retention problem?" I asked.

"It all breaks down into the two issues of recruiting and retention, but you have to look at the problem from both perspectives," he added. "I look at staffing like a house. Recruiting is the front door, and retention is the back door. We need to open the front door wider and bring more people in and shut the back door to keep people from leaving. And retention is the easier one to talk about."

So, I asked him to talk about it. "What are your ideas for retention? Why do officers leave, and what can be done about it?"

> Officers are retiring as soon as they're eligible, which is twenty years of service, and younger officers aren't being mentored properly.

"In New York, several things could be done at the state level, but I'm not sure that people are there yet. Number one, there's a thing in some cities called the DROP program, which is a deferred retirement option. Essentially, it allows you to retire with your final average salary, and then you can come back to work. Let's say your pension in retirement is $100,000 per year. You go into the DROP program for three to five years, depending on how the local law is structured. The pension goes into a fund while an officer is in the program earning a salary, and at the end, they get the deferred pension in a lump sum, including interest. That kind of program would help us shut the back door."

I think this is an idea that needs to be looked at very seriously, especially in New York City, where retention is a major problem and recruitment is at an all-time low. Officers are retiring as soon as they're eligible, which is twenty years of service, and younger officers aren't being mentored properly. Keeping the older officers would increase the overall number of cops and provide guidance and instruction for newer recruits, but officers who reach retirement age need incentives to stay.

Rusin continued, "The next issue is Tier Six in the pension program, which only allows an officer a certain amount of overtime to count toward their pension." (As I learned, *Tier Six* refers to members of the police and fire department who joined the retirement system in April 2012 or later.) "Tier Six only applies to the newer guys, who now say they don't want to work overtime; they'd rather get a second job. Lack of overtime negatively affects recruitment, since pension is one of the attractive points of the job."

I understood the economic reasoning behind Tier Six, but the result shows an example of 'unintended consequences.'

"You're going to see police departments try to offer longevity pay to veteran officers," Rusin went on, "and the numbers will look astronomical to the taxpayers. If I weren't in this position, I'd think it's a crazy idea. But if we don't keep those twenty-year veterans for twenty-five or thirty years, we lose a lot of the demeanor and experience of dealing with the community and investigating crimes."

I recalled the days when I was coming of age, and some of my people I knew in the neighborhood would put their names on civil servant "lists," sometimes waiting years to be "called." And now there was this recruitment issue? "Is it just not cool to be a cop anymore?" I asked.

"I think that's problem number two: recruiting," Rusin answered. "What we've gone through over the past five to seven years has taken away some of the glamor of being in the policing world. I think there needs to be a reckoning of what the profession looks like when people talk to their kids."

I pointed out that he was voicing one of the reasons I set out to write this book. "I want to see and present an accurate picture of policing, and not just the negative aspects that get over-featured in the press," I explained. "It seems like the police and the media today are afraid to say anything positive. The police used to have good public relations when you did good police work—you could talk about your wins. Now, there's no talking about wins; it seems like the only police news is bad news. When one cop does something wrong anywhere in the country, it's all of you."

He nodded and added, "Everybody who wears blue. Recruitment is a national problem. There's going to have to be a national campaign."

"Like the Army and Navy, with advertising?"

"Exactly," Rusin replied. "If we don't do it and the numbers continue in the direction they're going, we're going to have to start cutting services."

"What does that mean?" I asked.

"We won't be able to respond to certain calls. We won't come to specific kinds of disputes anymore. And that's not going to go over well with the public."

We talked about recruiting initiatives and how local police departments do events and promotional videos, but Deputy

Chief Rusin was right about the recruitment problem needing a national solution.

I was hearing Mark Rusin's take from an administrator's viewpoint. Now, I wanted to know about his experiences as a cop. "What can you tell me about that?" I asked.

"I was fortunate enough to go to investigations early in my career," he told me.

"That's detective work?"

"Yes. I had only a couple of years on the job," Rusin said, "but all I ever wanted to do was interview people. I got to work with a great team."

"Do any particular cases come to mind?" I prompted.

"Probably the most famous case was the Baby Maddox case," Rusin said. "I was driving from Rochester to Syracuse when the Amber Alert went off."

Baby Maddox was a beautiful twenty-one-month-old child who had overcome a rare form of cancer and, in 2016, was found dead, dumped in Onondaga Creek near Syracuse.

"We found the father who had horrifically murdered his daughter," Rusin clarified. "He denied it over and over and finally broke."

"How do you talk to someone like that?" I had to ask. "How does he keep denying it, and how do you get him to admit it?"

"I always talked to the people I interviewed the same way I'm talking to you," he explained. "There's no difference in tone or tenor. Sometimes, you have to look at your volume control differently, but you have to be natural and empathetic to some degree. Of course, it's hard to have empathy with a guy who just murdered his daughter, but if you don't, and they see that you don't, they'll never give it up to you." He paused and then added, "I'm very proud of the confessions we got as a team."

For the purposes of this book, I needed more information about what was happening now, particularly regarding retention, training, and exercising good judgment. We talked about how lack of experience impacts judgment, particularly when trying to de-escalate situations.

"Take the guys you rode with last night," Rusin said. "These are younger officers with several years of good experience under their belts. But can you imagine an athlete going directly into the major leagues from high school? It's been done, but it's not how it's done. Most people need development."

I thought about that a moment as he continued, "We take our youngest people, twenty-one or twenty-two years old, and we put them out at midnight in the middle of the worst neighborhoods. We have a lot of young people who can make good decisions, but it's an unreasonable expectation to think they can do it every time. It's just not always going to go right. There's not enough experience or enough training. I think that very rarely are the mistakes of malicious intent—I think most of the time it's a judgment call where there just isn't the training or experience to get it right."

I thought about Verbal Judo and how effective it can be, and then what one of the officers had said the night before about different ways to de-escalate a situation: "Officers today are more hesitant to use force, even necessary force, as a de-escalation tool. The public doesn't understand that talking isn't always de-escalation. If a person poses an imminent threat, sometimes they need to be put on the ground and handcuffed. That can be a de-escalation, not excessive force."

It all comes down to judgment, but it seems the more tools and training an officer has, the better the judgment. I asked Rusin what issues challenge his officers' ability to do their jobs.

"The de-institutionalization of mental health facilities has been a problem for a long time now," Rusin answered. He explained that, at one time, individuals with mental health issues went to hospitals where they were regulated, medicated, and given a program to follow. With the closing of most mental health facilities in the 1970s, that regulation started to happen in jails. "Now," he said, "one consequence of bail reform is that people aren't going to jail to be regulated anymore. I'm not saying that jail is the right place. I'm saying that jail was the place because there wasn't any place else."

> It all comes down to judgment, but it seems the more tools and training an officer has, the better the judgment.

I asked him to say more about bail reform, a series of programs that look at alternatives to cash bail, including home confinement and conditional release.

"It might work for a percentage of the population," Rusin said, "like an offender arrested for drug possession who has a job or a family to care for, so I can't say it doesn't work at all, but there are a lot of instances where bail reform doesn't work. I don't think anyone considered the mental health aspect, for example."

He brought up the problem of petty larceny, specifically shoplifting. "A guy goes into the mall, steals a bunch of stuff, and we give him an appearance ticket, a summons to appear in court. The next day, he goes back, steals more stuff, and gets another ticket. You might not see that as a big problem, but we have major retailers closing down in impoverished areas because of theft, and citizens can't get the things they need, including prescriptions. This is the collateral damage of bail reform and staffing cuts: people think they can keep getting away with things without going to jail."

We discussed those unfortunate circumstances a bit more and then circled back to the training issue. I asked, "With your ranks being filled with younger, less experienced officers, is there enough training before these officers go out onto the street?"

Deputy Chief Rusin paused to consider. "Look at a Division One sports program and the money that goes into equipment and training. If I had that budget, I could do anything," he said. "You get your initial six-month academy training, then you go out and do three or four months of field training, and then there are forty hours of in-service training a year. Again, can you imagine being in any division sports program and training forty hours a year?"

He made it clear: the training could be better.

I had one more question for Rusin. "I'm coming from riding around in New York City, and I've met cops who are assigned to one task: looking for guns. Are guns a big problem in Syracuse?" I asked.

"Oh, yeah," Rusin said. "When you look at all the metrics—shootings, shots fired, gun homicides, guns recovered—it's all a major problem. We're well over twenty homicides a year. For a city of a hundred and forty thousand people, that's a very high number. Our mayor has prioritized this, and we're moving in the right direction."

I came away from my meeting with Mark Rusin with some answers to the most pressing questions. Maybe not immediate solutions, but intelligent, honest answers. I appreciated the authenticity of Deputy Commissioner Rusin. I didn't see a lot of action in Syracuse (which was probably a good thing), but I learned a lot, and I was satisfied with what I had learned.

CHAPTER 9

Intermission • *Connecting the Dots*

The power of community policing is in the relationship. This can happen only if an officer sticks around for a while.

—Father Gregory Boyle, Catholic priest and former gang member[6]

At this point in the journey, I couldn't avoid seeing some patterns everywhere I went. A steady current of domestic violence and unresolved mental health issues, in both the big city and the small, runs under a general environment where people just can't get along with each other, whether it's a woman breaking into her brother's house or husbands and wives calling the cops on each other. They can't get along in the house and can't get along with their neighbors. Interpersonal disputes are a big part of what the police deal with on an hourly basis.

In many of the situations I witnessed during my ride-alongs, nobody was committing any actual crimes. Call after call came through, mostly for the officers to respond and

---

6 Gregory J. Boyle, "LAPD Must Drop CRASH in Order to Regain Public's Trust," *Los Angeles Times,* September 27, 1999, https://www.latimes.com/archives/la-xpm-1999-sep-27-me-14666-story.html.

attempt to defuse individual and community conflict, which takes up an incredible amount of the police officers' time and effort. When communities stop being communities, it's the cops who end up picking up the pieces. Of course, they have to deal with this stuff, especially in the wake of how society has changed the way it addresses mental health, and often because the potential for escalation from a verbal argument to something physical is high. Still, it seems that some of the issues dropped into the police officers' laps could be handled more effectively elsewhere.

When it comes to mental health, wealthy people and even middle-class individuals have resources. Poor people don't. When state agencies largely abandoned mental health services in the 1970s and 1980s following the withdrawal of the federal government's financial support in 1965, they had no idea what effect it would have on the street. Well, now we know, and somehow, those services need to be restored.

> Every time I rode around in a police car, I found that most of what the officers were doing was pacifying conflict.

Every time I rode around in a police car, I found that most of what the officers were doing was pacifying conflict. They weren't stopping robberies or investigating actual crimes when they had to stop couples or neighbors from beating each other up. On one Brooklyn ride-along, a call had come in from a woman who said her husband was trying to kill himself. Once we got there, the man seemed fine, but who knew? The officers started talking to him, and the man became angry as he told the officers that his "baby mama called the police" on him.

You couldn't blame the woman; she was scared, right?

The guy became more and more agitated, getting really loud and belligerent, and protocol dictates that the police must call EMS and take him to the hospital for a psychiatric evaluation. That's the law: they either call EMS or they arrest him.

The officers found themselves in a game of "he said, she said." She said he was trying to kill himself. He said she was lying. The police looked for a gun. There was no gun.

Before the ambulance arrived, the man calmed down and offered to leave. "She don't want me here, I'll go. I'm fine."

The woman told police she was okay with that, but it was too late; she had called 911, and protocol says the police have to follow through, take the man to the hospital, and wait for an evaluation.

Was she telling the truth? Was he? Should cops have to spend two or more hours dealing with people who can't give each other the respect of leaving, cooling down, or cooperating somehow?

I saw this kind of conflict time and time again—in Brooklyn, the Bronx, Manhattan, and Syracuse. It looked like so much of modern policing is dealing with people's personal problems, and the protocols established by the law give them minimal leeway for judgment because there can always be that exception—that one time when the guy *does* have a gun and uses it.

The breakdown in mental health services also led to an extreme increase in the homeless population. It is estimated that, as of April 2024, there are at least 350,000 unhoused people in New York City, according to the Coalition for the Homeless.[7]

---

[7] "State of the Homeless 2024: The Scope of Homelessness in NYC," Coalition for the Homeless, accessed March 3, 2025, https://www.coalition forthehomeless.org/state-of-the-homeless-2024/#the-scope-of-homelessness-in-nyc.

INTERMISSION · CONNECTING THE DOTS

While there's a significant number of homeless people who legitimately lost their homes due to financial crises, there are a lot of people on the street who would, before the closing of psychiatric facilities, have been hospitalized. Studies show that the large majority of unsheltered homeless New Yorkers are people living with mental illness or other severe health problems.[8] Many of these are the people who went from being stabilized in mental health centers to being stabilized in jails (and then returned to the streets) and are now not stabilized at all.

I noticed other things about the low-income neighborhoods: the retail balance is different. Laundromats, barbers, liquor stores, and Chinese takeout places proliferate. There are very few retail chains and no banks. I couldn't find a bank anywhere, but there were a hell of a lot of check-cashing joints. And because they are fearful, most business owners close shop by eight o'clock.

Even more questions arose: What kind of training do new officers get before facing the streets? What do legal professionals and community leaders have to say about the current state of policing? And, most importantly, are there any solutions to the problems I'd been witnessing?

It was time to dig deeper and learn more about the NYPD—how they are trained and what happens behind the scenes.

---

[8] "New York City Homelessness: The Basic Facts," Coalition for the Homeless, updated May 2021, https://www.coalitionforthehomeless.org/wp-content/uploads/2021/05/NYCHomelessnessFact-Sheet3-2021_citations.pdf.

CHAPTER 10

The Academy · *Part One*

Hire character. Train skill.
—Peter Schutz, former president and CEO of Porsche

Community leaders told me they feel that police officers don't get enough training. Even the Deputy Chief of the Syracuse Police said there isn't enough training. Can that be true? What kind of training do police officers receive? How much training do they get? Who's doing the training? How about follow-up or in-service training?

The place to start getting answers had to be the NYPD Police Academy.

The Academy is a 750,000-square-foot structure on a sprawling 32-acre campus in College Point, Queens. Just to give you an idea of its size, the average Walmart Supercenter is 179,000 square feet. The Academy was opened in 2015, making it one of the NYPD's newest facilities.

It's not easy to get into the Police Academy. The hiring process can take months. Applicants must have sixty college credits or two years of active military service. They must be U.S. citizens, have a New York driver's license, and live in New York City or one of six counties close to the city within thirty days of hiring. Then there's the written entrance exam, the medical exam, the written and oral psychological exams, and the background character investigation—and, of course, drug and alcohol screenings.

The New York City Police Academy in College Point, Queens

I arrived at the Academy on the morning of December 8, 2023, and I had been instructed to arrive by 0630—that's 6:30 a.m. in military time. I was on time.

I headed from the parking lot to the main building, where 390 cadets comprising about half the cadet population, a mix of young men and women, were lined up outside in full-dress uniforms. The sun was rising, silhouetting what looked like the formation of a small army. I met Lieutenant DuVaughn Clacken, who explained that this was a daily assembly usually featuring military-style drills.

The cadets train in three trimesters of two months each. This day in December was the end of the trimester, so there was no drilling. The schedule was 1) assemble, 2) eat breakfast, and 3) sit for an exam at 8:30 a.m. Cadets take three 100-question multiple choice exams. To graduate, cadets must pass all three, with a passing grade of at least 70.

Cadets Assembly

My guide for the day was Sergeant Catherine Kunst, who would walk me through the typical day of a cadet, beginning with background on the curriculum. Sergeant Kunst, who has been with the NYPD since 2007, also taught me a lot about policing in general.

"There are three disciplines," she explained as we walked through the cafeteria, where breakfast was being served to a line of hungry cadets carrying trays. "Police science, law, and social science. Cadets are trained in all three."

I asked which was the hardest to learn.

"Law is, by far, the most difficult one to comprehend. What you think is the law is probably not the law we teach. You have to separate what you thought the law was the whole time."

Sergeant Kunst cited the example of burglary, explaining

that many people might define it as simply breaking into somebody's house and stealing something. But what the cadets learn is much more detailed and specific—the true letter of the law. Burglary is actually defined as *entering a dwelling with intent to commit any crime*. "That means if I come into your house, break your laptop, and climb back out the window, I'm still getting charged with burglary," Sergeant Kunst explained. "That's hard to comprehend because of what we've been told our whole lives about burglary."

"What is it called if I reach over and take that pen out of your pocket?" I asked.

"That's larceny," she said. "You take it off my person. But if you hit me in the face and take the pen, now it's a robbery."

"And the robbery is a more serious offense?" I asked.

"Absolutely, because there's a violent component."

> As we walked through classrooms and hallways, I got the sense that Sergeant Kunst knew every cadet and every instructor, and everyone knew her.

It was impressive how quickly the sergeant fired off answers to my questions about laws and the degrees of them. I couldn't help but want to pick her brain further. It quickly became apparent that her people skills and attention to detail made her a centerpiece of the Academy. As we walked through classrooms and hallways, I got the sense that Sergeant Kunst knew every cadet and every instructor, and everyone knew her.

"I make it a point to know people's names," she said. "If you call somebody by their first name in a place like this, they're blown away. It's the little details."

A cadet passing by caught the tail of our conversation and commented about Sergeant Kunst, saying, "Best sergeant in the place."

I found the cadet's positive attitude striking, and setting such a tone is the responsibility of sergeants like Kunst.

"This is the most rewarding spot in the police department," she said. "They adapt to my attitude and my perception of the department. If I say, 'The job sucks,' you're going to have a cadet spend six months, weekends off, getting paid to work out and sit in class, saying, 'This job sucks.'"

In my business and my publishing career, I have spent the most time discussing success and attitude and the relationship they have with one another, so I couldn't help but think Sergeant Kunst was raising her cadets to know the same principles. She chuckled when I suggested so.

"Absolutely," she said. "I have a four-year-old and a seven-year-old at home, and I use the same tactics at home and at work."

We turned the corner toward the gymnasium, and two more cadets greeted us with smiles.

After a short pause, Sergeant Kunst continued, "I tell these guys it took me fifteen years to get to a great spot like this. Nobody forgets their instructor. Chiefs come and go, commissioners come and go, but if you ask the cop with the most time on the job, 'Who was your instructor?' they're going to answer immediately. If an instructor gives a hundred percent to them, the cadets emulate that; they give it back to you. That's what I love so much about this position."

Catherine Kunst had also spent four years with the Strategic Response Group (SRG) of the NYPD, which then-Commissioner Bill Bratton formed for counterterrorism and the policing of political protests. I discuss SRG in more detail in Chapter 17.

"I was in SRG in 2020 during the demonstrations," she said.

In 2020, the SRG was under fire from several organizations, including Human Rights Watch and the New York Civil Liberties Union, who thought their actions were too extreme during the George Floyd protests. The Civil Liberties Union described the SRG's actions as "brutality."

"It was a very taxing time for us," she added. "Still, I thoroughly enjoyed my experience in SRG. They always made training a priority, and it was a tight-knit crew of officers, bonding over doing work that most police officers loathe—disorder control and dealing with unruly crowds."

Sergeant Kunst is also a member of the Police Organization Providing Peer Assistance (POPPA). The organization was established in 1996 in response to the suicides of twenty-eight police officers over a three-year period. POPPA consists of volunteer peers. Two hundred officers of all ranks specially trained in counseling techniques offer support to uniformed members and retirees who find themselves struggling. They are available 24/7.

> During my ride-alongs and discussions with community leaders, it became clear that there was a disconnect between the police and community members that kept both parties isolated.

"How busy is POPPA?" I asked.

"Oh, it's busy. It was especially busy during 2020. Cops call, saying things like, 'My friends don't understand what goes on, and I have nobody to talk to.' Talking to another cop makes a difference."

During my ride-alongs and discussions with community leaders, it became clear that there was a disconnect between the police and community members that kept both parties isolated. I hadn't considered that police felt isolated in their personal lives with friends and family to the extent that they would call upon POPPA. I wanted to know how officers are trained to deal with all the issues I saw on the street and whether their training is enough to bridge the gaps between them and the citizens.

Sergeant Kunst lauded the work of former Commissioner Bill Bratton, who cowrote the book on modern policing titled *The Profession: A Memoir of Community, Race, and the Arc of Policing in America* and who supported the broken windows theory. This theory, first studied by Stanford University psychologist Philip Zimbardo and introduced by George Kelling and James Wilson in 1982, posits that visible markers of disorder, such as vandalism, loitering, and broken windows, invite criminal activity and should be prosecuted. The theory was famously implemented by New York City Mayor Rudolph Guiliani in the 1990s. The theory has many supporters and critics, and therefore its effectiveness remains unproven and quite controversial. Sergeant Kunst's experience suggests the theory is worth examining.

"About a year ago," she said, "we had two cops on foot patrol, watching these men gambling, playing dice on the street. One of the players was carrying a firearm, adjusted it, and ended up shooting himself in the leg. 'What were you thinking, carrying a gun?' one of the cops said as they waited for the medics. And the guy says, 'Well, the cops weren't doing anything about us shooting dice, so I figure why not bring my gun out?' That is the broken windows theory proved as it's happening!"

I thought about my very first ride at the Four-Six, where there was a minor crime on every street. "Cops would be arresting people all day for small stuff and missing bigger crimes," I said, wondering whether the concept of broken windows theory just couldn't fit every mold.

"We teach prioritization and logic," she answered. "Use logic. Know when to walk away. Walking away doesn't make you weak. Using your brain is strength. Cops need to learn to choose their battles, which is an argument for having more mature cops."

Prioritization was one of the main themes of my time with the Four-Six, and so was the problem of younger cops not understanding the art of de-escalation, which I witnessed in Syracuse, particularly with inter-relational issues making up the majority of calls across the city and Upstate.

"I saw a lot of domestic violence problems and people out there who are not in great shape mentally," I shared with the sergeant. "How much training takes place to deal with that? Is there more than there used to be?"

"Use logic. Know when to walk away. Walking away doesn't make you weak. Using your brain is strength. Cops need to learn to choose their battles, which is an argument for having more mature cops."

"One of our disciplines is social science. *Domestic violence* is one chapter. *Juveniles* is one chapter. *People in crisis* is another. That's part of the Academy training," explained Sergeant Kunst. "When cadets graduate, they can come back for in-service training called Critical Incident Training (CIT). That's a three-day course on dealing with people in crisis, domestic, and mental health issues.

"I tell my students that the two most dangerous situations in the world for a cop are car stops and domestic violence incidents. Car stops, because you don't have X-ray vision, and you don't know what's in that car. Domestics, because the wife may say, 'Lock him up,' and the next thing you know, she's jumping on your back, screaming, 'Why are you taking my husband?' It happened to me!"

The possible scenarios that police face are infinite, and I wonder if all the training in the world could tackle all of them and how that training could get done. The idea of mandatory continuing education or "in-service" classes seemed like a start. But just a start. I thought about all the calls from Central regarding mental health issues and asked the sergeant, "Should there be specific 'mental health police'?" I asked. "Specially trained officers to go along on domestic calls?"

"The Academy has emergency service training," she replied. "They go to a one-week course at John Jay College of Criminal Justice. It's an amazing course on how to speak to people in crisis."

That sounded great but didn't quite answer the question, so I got more specific: "The mental health situation in the city is a large and concerning problem. The police are overwhelmed. Is there a solution to that? Should mental health even be under the umbrella of the police?"

Sergeant Kunst sighed. "Mr. Steiner, my best friend is a social worker, and we go over this all the time. I say, 'They're homeless.' She says, 'They're homeless because they're mentally ill.' We go back and forth." She lowered her voice. "There's such a preponderance of violence among the mentally ill; I'm not saying everyone, but the number is high. So, yes, you have to have the police involved. That's my personal opinion."

Next, I asked the ultimate question about training to a person in charge of training. "Should the police have more direct support when they're getting involved, or do they just need more training?"

In her trademark rapid response, Sergeant Kunst answered, "We can sit here and tell you what to say to somebody, but until you gain the experience, that's really when you learn."

Experience being the ultimate teacher was something I had heard over again in all my ride-alongs and in conversations with community leaders. And gaining experience means being mentored by those with more experience and being "brought into" the communities.

Then Sergeant Kunst shared a personal story. "When I started, I was a twenty-two-year-old girl from Long Island," she said. "I wasn't used to people not respecting the police. I always thought, you're a cop, people listen to you. I had a very difficult time. I had a lot of complaints put against me. I didn't know how to speak to people. I went into a community I wasn't familiar with. I didn't know how it operated, and I had a very hard transition. It wasn't until somebody who had twenty years on took me aside and told me, 'You have the right attitude. You have the heart to do this. But you're doing it incorrectly.' He taught me how to police smarter, not harder. We became partners, and I never got another force complaint. He told me there's so much you can do with your words and, more importantly, your tone."

I appreciated that she had shared this insight and told her so before she continued, "So, knowing that, and knowing that these young cadets don't have even as much social interaction as we did growing up, I make them stand in front of the class and talk. I want these guys to get used to being in a room with somebody and having a dialogue."

I understood what she was saying, but I had to point out, "I've ridden around with a lot of young police officers now, and almost all of them were good communicators. But some of these domestic disputes were way over even my head, and I've been around the block a few times!"

"Look," she said, "I've been a happily married woman for eleven years. If I get a twenty-two-year-old kid showing up at my door, what the hell is he going to tell me about my marriage? How is he going to help? But the other side of the coin is, if you have the cops coming to your door, you obviously need some kind of help."

A New Way to Recruit

We stopped our tour for a moment so I could be introduced to Lieutenant Khagay Ruvinov, who runs the Cadet Corps. We shook hands.

"Cadet Corps is college-level," explained Ruvinov. "We want to bring in people who have education, so we accept full-time students, give them jobs, and pay their tuition for two years, and in return, they give us two years of service in the department."

"Sort of like what the military does," I said.

He nodded. "It's a paid internship."

This was interesting. "Do you focus on particular schools?"

"Not really," he answered. "We're open to all the schools in New York City and Nassau and Westchester counties, all the two-year and four-year schools."

I hadn't known about the Cadet Corps. It's wise to recruit college students, even as short-timers, and perhaps they'll stay. *At least something is being done to address the recruitment dilemma,* I thought.

THE ACADEMY · PART ONE

The Robert Peel Steps at the New York City Police Academy

Sergeant Kunst and I continued our conversation, which quickly became a history lesson, as we approached a fifteen-step staircase, which boasted engraved words—the first five principles of Sir Robert Peel's Nine Principles of Policing:

1. The basic mission for which the police exist is to prevent crime and disorder.

2. The ability of the police to perform their duties depends on public approval of police actions.

3. Police must secure the willing cooperation of the public in voluntary observance of the law to be able to secure and maintain the respect of the public.

4. The degree of cooperation of the public that can be secured diminishes proportionately to the necessity to use physical force.

5. Police seek and preserve public favor not by catering to public opinion but by constantly demonstrating absolute impartial service to the law.

At the time, I didn't know who Sir Robert Peel was. The sergeant explained that he was prime minister of Britain twice, and in 1829, he founded London's Metropolitan Police Force. Peel, whose nickname was Bob, is known as the father of modern policing.

"Do you know why they call English police *Bobbies*?" Sergeant Kunst asked me.

I shook my head.

"It's in his honor."

We entered the Academy gym, which was inspiring and impressive, boasting a track (twelve laps equals 1.5 miles) and a regulation basketball court.

"Cadets use the gym for an hour during their break or first thing in the morning. They have time for laps, calisthenics, and weights, then they change their shirts and do an hour-and-a-half of tactics."

Tactics include defensive methods, using both the straight baton and the expandable baton, frisking and cuffing, first aid, cardiopulmonary resuscitation, and water-safety skills.

Firearms training, which is separate from tactics, is a five-week course. It begins with five days of basic firearms instruction consisting of the introduction to the gun and the art of shooting. On the fifth day, cadets qualify on the range. If they pass, they move on to four weeks of tactical firearms training: close combat, how to enter a room, and car stops.

"Where does basketball come in?" I asked.

"The community, Mr. Steiner. They play basketball here on the weekends."

Sergeant Kunst introduced me to one of the gym instructors, Sergeant Jamie Blandeburgo. I explained to her a little of what I was doing there. I asked her about the importance of physical conditioning—specifically if she thought cops should have more, especially throughout their careers.

"I feel like there should be more [physical and tactical training]," she answered, "because you're dealing with people on the streets who have less respect for us than they used to."

Basic Training Gym

I took that to mean there was more potential for physical altercations than there had been in the past. "Why do you think that is?" I asked.

"I think that's part of what the city has done. Letting people out—they're getting arrested and walking out an hour later, committing the same crime. Society itself has less respect for the police."

> "Society itself has less respect for the police."

I wasn't sure that physical training was a solution to the respect problem, but I agreed with the sentiment itself. "Do cops come back for additional tactical training?"

"We do it within the six months that they're here in the Academy," she said. "But I think police officers should keep up with their health and wellness. Working out improves your health, helps you feel better, work better, act better, think better, so I think they should be doing it on their own."

"So, while you have them for six months," I asked, "how much physical training do they get?"

"We get them for about two-and-a-half hours a day," Sergeant Blandeburgo answered. "It's not every single day, but it is most days."

"And how many people are in your unit at the gym?"

"We have eighteen officers and detectives instructing, between day tour and four to twelve. "Officers work in three shifts. The day tour is from eight a.m. to four p.m.

I asked Sergeant Blandeburgo how long she'd been with the police. She told me she was coming up on twenty years on the force. "I'm at the tail end of my career."

I shared my personal anecdotal knowledge of seeing too

many people leaving the police department at their peak of knowledge and experience. "It looks like officers are retiring and taking other jobs. Why not stay on the job where what you know has the most value?"

She smiled. "Were you a cop?" she asked me.

I laughed. "I'm a businessman, but I got this idea from a deputy chief in Syracuse. He was brilliant and really into thinking about retention."

I understood not to prompt further, and Sergeant Kunst changed the subject. She spoke about some of the challenges of training young recruits. "We try to explain to them that what they get here in this training facility is completely different from what they're going to face in the streets. They need to be prepared for whatever is coming at them, and it's hard to prepare them in six months."

I wondered if they should get more than six months' training or if they might create on-the-job training modules, the way teachers and nurses learn as they work—more mandatory in-service continuing education, including physical and tactical training, perhaps. While the Academy has a first-rate gym and the cadets are encouraged to work out, once they leave the Academy, fitness isn't necessarily as much of a priority as it should be. The sergeant and I talked about how, with the help of the Police Benevolent Association (their union) and the Police Foundation, the gyms at many precincts had been upgraded, but more still needed to be done to encourage the officers to stay in good physical shape.

Sergeant Blandeburgo spoke at length about the difficulty in trying to keep officers fit once they leave the Academy. "They're going to graduate, go on to four-to-twelve shifts or onto midnights, they're not going to sleep right, they're not going to eat right, they'll gain weight, and once they have kids, they'll never go to the gym."

"Then how do you convince them to develop and keep good habits?" I asked.

"It's hard," the sergeant said. "We have charts, guest lectures on nutrition, and we make them aware of the statistics of heart attacks among police officers, but it's not easy to get people to change. We do our best to instill good habits, but the department needs to come up with a way to entice officers to work out."

Being a sports-oriented guy, I was glad to see the Academy's emphasis on fitness and the instructors' dedication. As I left the gym to head to my next destination, my only disappointment was that I didn't get to play any basketball.

CHAPTER 11

The Academy · *Part Two*

If you can't think to do it in training, what makes you think you'll think to do it in the street?

—Tony Blauer, former U.S. Marine and world-renowned self-defense and fear management expert.

Touring the very beginning of the police pipeline enabled me to broaden my ideas of what the NYPD encompassed. It was training, both physical and tactical. It was educational, including providing internships to college students. It was social and legal, with the acknowledgment that training should not just be a one-and-done—graduate and then police—but an ongoing experiential journey.

The layers kept peeling away as I met with other training officers, like Officer Brian Rao, who was not only a training officer at the Academy but a member of GOAL-NY, Gay Officers Action League. The Gay Officers Action League (GOAL) is a pioneering organization established in 1982 to address the needs and concerns of gay and lesbian law enforcement personnel. GOAL was founded by Charles Henry "Charlie" Cochrane, Jr. (August 5, 1943–May 5, 2008), a sergeant of the New York City Police Department.

After delivering public testimony on anti-gay discrimination legislation pending before the New York City Council in 1981, Cochrane became the first openly gay officer of the NYPD. Since its inception as a fraternal organization, GOAL has advocated for the rights of its members and assisted them with issues of discrimination, harassment, and disparate treatment in the workplace. The organization offers a forum for members to discuss their needs and concerns in a supportive environment without fear of job-related reprisals.

On the force for over twenty years, Officer Rao was gracious enough to discuss his experiences with me. I noted his willingness to talk in the hallway instead of someplace more private.

"When you started, did you let people know you were gay?" I asked.

"I was in the closet," he said. "No one knew. My family did not know."

"How," I asked, "did your coming out happen?"

Officer Rao paused and began to share his story. "I was married to a female, and I had no desire to be a gay man in society. None. Zero. I'm from Long Island, and when I started working in the city in 2003 and saw that there were 'normal' gay people living here, leading a normal existence, I said, 'Wow, it's possible.' As I started hanging out in that community, that's when I decided to come out of the closet. But I didn't come out at work. I told my ex-wife and my family, but I didn't tell anyone at work for another three or four years, in 2007."

So, now that Officer Rao had been living and working openly as gay for the last seventeen years, I wondered if he thought it had gotten more acceptable in the police department, even in such a relatively short period of time.

"It's definitely better," he answered, "but there are still . . . things. I just try to handle those things with a sense of humor, so if I hear statements that are inappropriate, I try to speak to those things in a more appropriate way."

"As a trainer, I assume you try to increase the knowledge among your students about these issues to try to help the heterosexual officers to be less discriminatory?"

"Yes, that's a big part of it," said Officer Rao. "I teach a class here four times a year, a workshop on sensitivity toward the LGBTQ community. I'm very proud of that class; it's excellent."

"Did you create the class?"

"No, the department did. Of course, I put my own spin on it."

I told him that I generally see cohesiveness in the precincts I've visited. Officers seemed to be tight, regardless of color, gender, or sexual orientation.

"I try to teach my students to embrace our stereotypes," Rao explained. "Embrace the fact that we can be made fun of for them. To me, the best part of the job is the camaraderie we have with our brothers and sisters. And what do brothers and sisters do? They make fun of each other. We need to learn to accept that we can make fun of each other for the things that are attached to us—not horribly racist or sexist things, but the funny things we tease each other about.

"I tell these guys, 'You're going to see some sick sh—t on this job, and the way to keep your sanity is through your sense of humor. When you see that sick sh—t, you have to start teasing each other just to balance your brain!'"

I had another question about Rao's personal experience. "What's the difference between now and when you first came out seventeen years ago?"

"Night and day," he answered. "Of course, my role is very different. Back then, I started in patrol and then narcotics. Now, I'm in an authoritative role. At this point, if they let on to me that they have a problem with gay people," he chuckled, "I can just torture them in the gym."

With my mind on recruitment, I asked, "Would you say

that there's more of an incentive for gay men and women to join the department now that it's more accepted?"

Rao told me that he'd known a few recruits who were more willing to join because of the change in culture. "Some recruits have come up to me and said that because of my influence, they feel more comfortable with the idea of coming out. That's amazing."

I was pleased to learn that the department was changing for the better, largely thanks to people like Brian Rao.

* * *

My next stop on my daylong tour of the Academy was the third floor, where the classrooms are located. Each classroom resembled a college lecture hall, with the desks arranged in tiered arcs facing the instructor below, a style of instruction I remembered well from my Syracuse days.

I sat in on an introductory class where an instructor explained how the trimesters are organized, where and how firearms training takes place, and what constitutes emergency vehicle driver training.

The driver training course, called EVOC (Emergency Vehicle Operator Course), is a four-day high-speed course at Floyd Bennett Field in Brooklyn. I know Floyd Bennett Field. When I was young, I drove past it every day. It's a vast space on the southern end of Flatbush Avenue that was an airfield long ago. I saw how it would be an excellent place for high-speed driving. I also thought about the officers I rode with in the Bronx as they drove full speed through the streets. Good to know those officers were trained!

The instructor also pointed out the military aspect of the training, which I had noticed all day. Groups of students assembled on the muster deck, and there was a lot of drilling, saluting, and chain-of-command stuff. Superior officers must be addressed as such and saluted, just like in the military.

"We're building discipline," the instructor explained to a full lecture hall with students looking head-on. "A student walks in a civilian, and we have six months to prepare them to be out on the street in a blue uniform, handling whatever comes up."

> "A student walks in a civilian, and we have six months to prepare them to be out on the street in a blue uniform, handling whatever comes up."

He then explained the scenario-based training unit. "That's where the recruits take what they learn in the classroom and apply it. We act out real scenes with actors and guided scenarios, and it feels like you're in a live environment."

The Academy simulates street scenes and even built a subway car into the Academy building. They have a courtroom (cops have to testify in court) for mock testimonies.

"Our attorneys teach that course," explained the instructor. "After the recruits get a lesson in class, they act it out in the scenario-based unit with the actors, and then they go to the courtroom a couple of weeks later to apply what they've learned in testimony about the scenario."

It had never occurred to me that officers would receive training on how to testify.

Then I asked, "What is a typical training day like?"

"A basic day for one of our recruits consists of three ninety-minute blocks in three subjects," the instructor replied. "One is social science, which includes behavioral science. Police science is all about procedure and what's in our Patrol Guide. The third subject is law, and that's the hardest and most important. After those three classes, there's a one-hour meal break, then a two-and-a-half-hour gym block. That's a standard eight-hour day."

The Job Standard Test (JST)

Earlier that day, my guide, Sergeant Kunst, had told me about a test that was in progress: The Job Standard Test, or JST. During the first week of the Academy, each recruit has to run a six-station obstacle course in 3:32 or less. Every recruit has to pass the JST once before they complete their training. They don't have to retake it if they pass it in week one, but fewer than half can do that.

According to the NYPD website:

> By the very nature of their work, police officers are asked to meet certain physical requirements. The NYPD's Job Standard Test is a physical endurance test to evaluate an applicant's ability to perform physical tasks typically associated with a routine radio call or a critical incident.

The six stations of the obstacle course are:

1. **Fence Surmount:** The candidates start on their knees, then sprint 50 feet to surmount a six-foot fence. It was a wall until 2022, when the department eased the requirement following a wave of increased retirements.

2. **Stair Climb:** Then, from the fence, the candidates proceed to run to a six-stair climb and climb up and down the stairs three times.

3. **Physical Restraint Simulation:** Next, they go from the Stair Climb to a push/pull machine. This tactics-and-training device simulates a struggle with an assailant.

4. **Pursuit Run:** Next, they run to a pattern of cones that provides twists and turns, where they run six laps (600 feet). By this point, their heart rate is up, and their breathing is getting shallow.

5. **Victim Rescue:** Now, it's a simulated victim rescue! They drag a 176-pound dummy a distance of 35 feet. That is one heavy dummy!

6. **Trigger Pull:** After all that, the candidates run to a trigger-pull station, pick up an inoperative firearm, and hold the firearm within a nine-inch diameter metal ring. Then, they pull the trigger sixteen times with the dominant hand and fifteen times with the nondominant hand. The firearm has to stay within the metal ring the whole time. If they touch the ring, they lose time. Timing stops upon completion of the final trigger pull.

Oh, by the way, they have to do this obstacle course wearing a fourteen-pound vest. Fourteen pounds doesn't sound like much until you pick it up. It's the same weight and the same test for men and women. I was glad I didn't have to take that test!

Beyond Basic

At the Academy later that day, I met some of the police divers. They weren't there for recruit training but for the specialized training that officers must have to join the elite NYPD SCUBA team, whose primary function is search and rescue. Their training also took place at the Academy.

The SCUBA divers must be in top physical condition, with eighteen months of certified dive experience. Their training includes comprehensive written and medical exams;

candidates are required to perform a minimum of twelve pull-ups, thirty-two pushups, seventy-five sitting tucks, a mile run in under six minutes forty-eight seconds, a 500-yard swim in under twelve minutes, a 25-yard underwater swim wearing a ten-pound weight belt, a fifty-minute survival float, and three minutes treading water using feet only.

I knew the police had divers, and I vaguely understood what they did. Still, I got to ask Detective Mark Kopystianskyj, a member of the SCUBA team, for information. Mark has been on the SCUBA team for thirteen years.

"How many people are in your unit?" I asked.

"About thirty," he answered. "For the whole city. Twenty-four hours a day, and that includes the SCUBA boat and the air-sea rescue helicopter."

"Do you guys look for bodies in the water?" I asked. "That sort of thing?"

"Yeah, if there's a body, we go down and get it, we help with helicopter rescue, and we do a lot of evidence recovery—guns in the water, knives in the water, ATMs, drugs, planes. We pull it all out."

I wondered about divers searching for weapons. "I think, if I were a criminal," I said, "I would either throw my gun down a sewer or into the water."

"A lot of guns get thrown in the water, yes. It would probably be easier to find one in the sewer. We probably find about twenty guns in the water per year."

Kopystianskyj explained that other divisions don't have their own divers—that the SCUBA team works with every group in the department, including Counterterrorism. "Diving is all we do, twenty-four-seven. So we'll dive bridge stanchions, power plants, etc."

One of the things that makes New York City unique is water. Manhattan is an island. Brooklyn and Queens are part of Long

Island. Staten Island is separated from the other boroughs by water. New York Harbor is one of the world's major seaports.

To carry through my observations on the need for better mental health responses, I wondered if SCUBA was involved with saving people from their despair. Being from a city where there are eighteen major bridges (out of a total of 789 bridges and tunnels), I wondered if Detective Kopystianskyj felt this was as serious an issue as I thought it was. "Are there as many people jumping off bridges as we hear stories about?" I asked.

"There are a lot more than you would expect," he said, his tone becoming softer. "Every day, there are a handful of calls—not necessarily people jumping off a bridge, but somebody up there attempting. Sometimes, ESU [Emergency Services Unit] is able to talk them down, or a cruising helicopter spots them, and as soon as the job comes over the radio, we come in. We're on the scene before a jump. SCUBA is on the water end, ESU is up top trying to rescue, and ninety-nine percent of the time, ESU talks them down. Still, there are a lot of attempts."

I nodded, thinking about how much work these divers do. "How much training does someone need to join your unit?"

"It's usually about eight to nine months, and applicants have to be a police officer for a minimum of three years to get into our unit."

"If you could tell everyone in New York City about your department, what would you want them to know?" I asked.

"That we work our butts off to help them every day," he said without hesitation. "We do the unseen work that nobody knows or appreciates, but every cop is killing themselves to keep everybody safe."

He was talking about every cop in the police department, but I pointed out that most citizens don't even realize that the SCUBA team exists.

"Most people don't," he agreed. "My team is all over the

city, from Coney Island and the Rockaways to City Island, the rivers—everywhere and anywhere we're needed."

The SCUBA team patrols the city, not in cars, but underwater.

The SCUBA team patrols the city, not in cars, but underwater.

Spackle and the Spectacle

There was one thing I kept thinking about as I toured this amazing facility: The current police academy opened in 2015. I wondered why the state-of-the-art quality of the Academy didn't carry over into the precincts. It seemed like nobody was even thinking of remodeling the precinct houses. Sergeant Kunst had been with me throughout the day, and I asked her about it.

"The SRG [Strategic Response Group 4] building that I worked in, right across the highway from here, was a former armory. It's a legit castle," she explained. "It's a beautiful façade with a great view. We used to go up on the roof all the time, but the interior of the building is dilapidated and doesn't accommodate the people it houses. For example, the job sometimes required working sixteen to eighteen hours straight, and there was no separate shower for female officers."

The Strategic Response Group (SRG) is the unit of the NYPD that addresses counterterrorism and the policing of political protests. I will discuss this unit more in chapter 17. I was surprised they didn't have an up-to-date facility to work out of.

"Look, I'm a mother," said Sergeant Kunst, "and I like to have a clean house. You can look at any study you want—people are going to be happier coming here to this beautiful facility. If I go to a police station that's dilapidated, falling apart, infested, and has no heat, of course, that affects me mentally!"

Strategic Response Group 4, Queens
(Photo courtesy of New York Adventure Club)

Instead of militarizing or defunding the police, we should think about finding ways to fund improvements to the police environment. I suggested that there might be a way to get Corporate America involved with sponsorships.

"That would be one way," Sergeant Kunst said. "SRG-One in Manhattan just got a brand-new facility, but that took a long time."

I was blown away earlier in the day when I learned that the Academy holds four graduation ceremonies a year—at Madison Square Garden, one of the most iconic places in the city. Champions play in that arena. The biggest events in New York take place there. The graduation itself, they tell me, is spectacular. In fact, one of the classroom instructors described it as a show: "You bring your family, everybody's in their dress blue uniform, there's a band. The mayor speaks, and the police commissioner. Any cop will tell you, the most memorable day is that day."

I thought about what happens after such an elaborate graduation—it would be a 180-degree turn when the new graduates enter a precinct station that needs some aesthetic attention.

NYPD Academy Graduation at Madison Square Garden

My day at the Police Academy opened my eyes to what the police in New York City do and how they learn to do it. There's a lot to urban policing that is invisible to most citizens. I'm grateful I had a chance to see this.

I get how it begins: learning law, social science, and police science. I'd been on the streets with police officers. I'd seen what recruits needed to do to become cops. Next, I wanted to know what else is behind the scenes of the NYPD—what the scientific side of policing was like.

It was time to visit the Crime Lab.

CHAPTER 12

The Crime Lab, *Part One—Guns*

Wherever he steps, whatever he touches, whatever he leaves, even unconsciously, will serve as silent evidence against him. This is evidence that does not forget.

—Dr. Paul Leland Kirk, biochemist and criminalist[9]

When we think of the police, we think of men and women in uniform who make traffic stops or patrol the streets. I've seen the cadets in training learning how to use firearms and being pushed to extend their physical limits as well as their knowledge of how to deal with civilians and how to make an arrest. But there is so much more than what we see. It's astonishing how much expertise, money, and people power it takes to do modern-day policing.

I began to learn about specialization on my ride-alongs when I accompanied officers who were tasked with finding guns or stolen vehicles or drugs. I learned more about specialization at the Academy when I met the SCUBA divers and the trainers specializing in firearms, physical training, or police science. Of course, I couldn't ride along with the "background" police officers, so when the rare opportunity came up to visit

---

[9] Paul Leland Kirk, *Crime Investigation* (Wiley, 1974), 2.

their workplaces and meet the people behind the scenes, I jumped at the chance. In this case, I'd be meeting with the detectives and scientists who work in the Crime Lab.

The NYPD Forensic Investigations Division, Queens

The NYPD Forensic Investigations Division Crime Laboratory in Jamaica, Queens, is the largest facility of its kind, both in size and staff, in the country, with more than 350 employees. There are five floors in the building, comprising the Drug Lab, Firearms, Fingerprint Development, and General Criminalistics, which is hair and fibers, paint comparison, etc. The staff is a combination of police and civilians.

Shortly after I walked in the door, I was greeted by the spirited Detective Matt Brady, who had been working in the Crime Lab since 2016. Detective Brady knew my face from the sports-related programs I used to host on the YES Network. I told him I wanted to understand what the Crime Lab does.

"Oh, everything," Detective Brady said, his voice enthusiastic. "You name it."

I asked him to explain.

"We have five floors altogether," he said, placing his suit jacket on the back of his desk chair. "On the top floor, they do drug analysis, determining whether it's cocaine, heroin, whatever."

I imagined the fifth floor was a busy one, since drugs were one of the prevailing issues I saw during the ride-alongs. "So, when you confiscate drugs, that's where you find out what kind of drug it is?" I asked.

"Yes," he replied and added with a slight chuckle, "We do everything you see on TV."

"But how is it different?" I asked, knowing that real life doesn't fit into an hourlong episode.

"Oh, there are some Hollywood-ifications," he said, wearing a grin, "such as turnaround times."

Of course, TV shows need to keep the story moving forward so results they get seem instantaneous to the viewers, but I was still curious about the comparison and asked, "On TV, when they take evidence from a crime scene 'to the lab' and come back with specific findings, is it like that?"

"It's kind of like that," Detective Brady answered. "When they dig the fibers out of a car seat and say, 'These fibers are consistent with . . .' it's not to the level that TV goes, where they say, 'These fibers were made by Sears Manufacturing in 1960.' No, it's not like that. But if we have samples taken from your car and we have samples from a body, we can show that the fibers are consistent with each other."

I would imagine that with all the incriminating evidence at the lab, not to mention the equipment and drugs, many criminals would kill to get their hands on the stuff. "Do you worry about anyone stealing from the lab?"

"Not here. It's a secure facility. We're staffed twenty-four seven, and all the doors are card access."

At that moment, Captain Matt Strong walked toward us. He had just come from the Firearms Unit in the basement of the Crime Lab, where about seventy-five people work, and introduced himself as he approached us.

I smiled as we shook hands and had to ask, "Did you take a lot of heat over that last name when you were a kid?"

"I took a lot of heat in the Academy," the captain answered, straight-faced, "when I was wearing STRONG across my chest and struggling on the fiftieth push-up!"

I chuckled. As we spoke, I learned that, along with Detective Brady, Captain Strong was assigned to the Firearms Analysis Section and that he had started with the NYPD in 2004.

"Our primary responsibility is to analyze firearms and firearms-related evidence," Detective Brady explained.

"When you say *analyze*," I asked, "are you trying to figure out *where* a gun came from or *who* made it?"

"Both, and how it was used."

Captain Strong offered to show me around the unit. He introduced me to Sergeant Billy Hempstead and Lieutenant Mike Bopp, also part of the Firearms Unit.

I pointed to a very old but impressive-looking machine gun on the wall. "Is there any particular reason that's hanging on the wall?"

"Because it looks great," Hempstead answered.

"Yeah, I need that in my office!" I agreed with a laugh. "But, really, does it have a particular meaning?"

"We used to have a sergeant here who was a World War I buff," Hempstead explained. "He put that Browning M1917 thirty-caliber machine gun up on the wall. It does send a certain message, doesn't it?"

Captain Strong next led me into a space with a long black

counter. "When guns come in," he explained, "the first stop is the gun floor. This is where the firearms team inventories and evaluates the guns as they arrive. They evaluate the firearms for safety and functionality, if they're safe to test-fire, or if there are any other issues we need to identify."

I looked at the profusion of tagged weapons on the table and on the shelves around me. "Are these all confiscated guns?"

"They could have been confiscated during an arrest, they could have been found in the street, or seized under a search warrant," Captain Strong explained. "Some of them might have even been surrendered."

"What does *surrender* mean?"

"Well, for instance, if you lose your license, you have to surrender . . . give up your firearm."

I learned that the ultimate goal of testing every firearm is to make sure it's safe to be test-fired. The lab test-fires guns to compare to other evidence and/or to compare its markings to guns used in earlier crimes.

> "If you get arrested with a firearm, in order to prosecute you, the gun has to work. If it doesn't work, it's a paperweight, and they won't be able to use it in court."

"We might find out that the gun you were arrested with was used in two homicides last year," explained Strong. "Also, if you get arrested with a firearm, in order to prosecute you, the gun has to work. If it doesn't work, it's a paperweight, and they won't be able to use it in court."

Strong showed me where a gun goes through function checks, safety checks, and inventory processes. "If the gun came in with ammunition, the ammunition gets inventoried. There are different criminal charges for a loaded firearm or an unloaded one."

I thought back to my discussion with Sergeant Kunst at the Academy about the depth and breadth of the law and how these officers have to be trained to know this kind of detail.

"So, first, we check to see if the firearm works," Strong elaborated, "and then we note whether it is loaded. I learned that each gun, no matter what shape it is in, can be deceiving and is handled with the utmost care." Strong continued, "Sometimes, we get a gun that's held together with duct tape or missing parts, with paper clips stuck in them to make them work, but if they work, then it's a useable firearm."

We climbed three metal stairs to a huge steel box that looked like a giant refrigeration unit lying on its side, with a big tube at one end. This was where the bullets were tested.

"This is a ballistic retrieval tank," Captain Strong explained. "Once all the checks are done, and it's safe to fire, the techs bring it in here, stand here by the tube, fire the gun through the tube down into the water in the tank. The water slows the bullet. . . . The bullet doesn't hit the wall and get damaged; it slows down in the water and drops. You end up with an intact bullet. Having a bullet that isn't damaged is helpful to the lab because it allows us to match bullets that have been fired earlier to the bullet we fired into the tank."

I listened carefully as Strong continued, "All guns except smooth bore rifles and shotguns have rifling in the barrel—little cuts that spin the bullet as it goes through, making the shot more accurate and leaving marks we can analyze on the bullet. Smooth bores don't have those little cuts. The bad thing about bullets we get in the field is that they hit a lot of things. The bullet hits the wall or the ground, and the bullet deforms, breaks, or shatters. Very rarely do we get an intact bullet from the field unless it comes from the morgue. So, the test-fire is as close to a true bullet as you can get, and we use that for comparison."

Ghost Guns

"How many guns are coming in here?" I asked. "What kind of volume?"

"Seven thousand a year," Strong said, and I was stunned. "It varies day-to-day. On a Monday morning when we come in, we usually get between a hundred to a hundred and fifty from over the weekend. Most are either found or arrest-confiscated.

"If there's a long case with a search warrant, like if they've been watching someone buying or selling a lot of guns, we get a heads-up. But we've had takedowns, especially when they were doing the ghost gun task forces, with forty or fifty guns all at once from a single case."

> Ghost guns, which are made from kits, don't have serial numbers.

Ghost guns, which are made from kits, don't have serial numbers. The people who manufacture these ghost guns often turn their apartments into workshops. Ghost gun kits contain plastic parts that, by themselves, aren't considered weapons. But put those parts together, and you've got an unregistered gun. The only way to trace them is by the casing marks. The lab keeps a record of those marks to determine if the same gun is used again.

Captain Strong estimated that they used to receive about fifty ghost guns a year, but lately the number had increased at a scary pace. "Five years ago," he said, "you'd see one or two ghost guns. Then you'd see ten, and then fifty, and then a hundred. Last year, we had seven hundred of them come through here."

Examples of ghost guns

"How did the ghost gun thing start?" I asked, since I hadn't heard of them until recently.

Strong explained, "A company out west kept sending stuff to the ATF [Bureau of Alcohol, Tobacco and Firearms], because it's up to the ATF to define whether an item is a gun or not. They asked, 'Is this a gun?' and every time the ATF said, 'Yes, that's a gun,' they'd take off a piece and send it back, until eventually the ATF said, 'No, this isn't a gun, it's a piece of plastic.' Then the company started selling those pieces of plastic, with tools and instructions for assembling them. So, they were selling unregistered guns, but you needed about an hour's worth of work and some mechanical skill to finish it."

I learned that the Bureau of Alcohol, Tobacco, and Firearms is responsible for tracking the interstate trafficking of guns. Strong elaborated, "If a gun that was stolen in Nebraska is recovered here, it's the ATF that investigates how that gun got from Nebraska to New York City. The pipeline is their responsibility."

> It was astonishing how people could put together guns like model airplanes and do so through the mail.

It was astonishing how people could put together guns like model airplanes and do so through the mail. I wondered what other out-of-the-ordinary things the unit saw. "So, what is a typical day here, and what would be considered unusual?"

"Unusual?" Strong said, pondering for a moment. "We've had guns explode. We had something come in from the Tenement Museum downtown. They were renovating a Lower East Side tenement that the museum owned." (The Tenement Museum preserves and displays the history of immigrant, migrant, and refugee families who settled in tenement apartments in New York City.) "They pulled up some floorboards and found a top-break revolver that was at least one hundred and fifty years old. The analyst spent a week trying to figure out who the manufacturer was and where the gun had come from. We're still not sure."

I thought again about the television shows and how the characters would know not only the manufacturer within minutes but also what crime was committed with it and why. In fact, we'd probably get a play-by-play in an old dream sequence.

Thinking some more, Strong added, "My first month here, we had an M-sixty machine gun come in, in parts. They did a search warrant on somebody's house and found a bucket of pieces. When we put the pieces together, it was a Brazilian replica of an M-sixty."

There's even a bazooka!

I was hearing a lot about firearms, but I wasn't seeing many. "Where are all these guns now?"

"I'll show you."

"They're all in one place?" I was stunned.

"No," Strong said. "Once we've analyzed the firearms and we're done with them, they go over to the property clerk, where they stay until the court cases are resolved. Then they're destroyed."

I discovered there is a room full of guns. It's really hard to get in. Key codes, cards, etc. If you're not authorized, you don't get in.

"This is evidence control," Captain Strong said as he unlocked a door with a code, and again I was stunned. *Thousands* of guns.

Long guns were laid out on tables—a hell of a lot of rifles and shotguns. I saw bins full of pistols and filing cabinets full of envelopes stuffed with bullets and shell casings.

"It seems like a lot of rifles," I remarked."

"This room turns over about every three days. All this will be gone and replaced with more stuff. Except these." He took me over to some stacks of boxes. "These are bullets and shell casings going back to the sixties."

"Why?"

"These are old evidence that the department doesn't want to be destroyed. There may be a cold case, or a suspect from a homicide in the eighties passes away. The family finds a gun in the house—we might have a match."

Being around such an arsenal was disconcerting, despite the security. "What's the most dangerous thing you've seen in your time here?" I asked.

He had a ready answer: "Three-D printed guns. The Feds and the State started restricting the manufacture and sale of gun parts, which limits ghost guns, but ghost guns were just the first iteration of the idea that you don't need to buy a commercially manufactured firearm. Now you don't even have to buy a kit; you can just use a 3D printer to print the parts yourself out of plastic!"

"They're cheap, I suppose?" I asked, learning that the prevalence of 3D printed guns has increased nationally from 8,500 in 2020 to 38,000 in 2024.

Machine guns.

THE CRIME LAB, PART ONE—GUNS

"Insanely cheap and completely untraceable," Strong said. "Also, insanely dangerous because there's no regulation of them. The people who are making 3D-printed guns aren't chemists. They don't know the strength of the plastics they're using, they don't understand the physics, and some of them explode."

We talked more about the increased number of guns on the street and how the end of the city's stop-and-frisk policy has added to that increase. The stop-and-frisk policy allowed police officers to temporarily detain, question, and search civilians and suspects on the street for weapons and other contraband. Because of complaints of racial profiling, in 2013, the courts determined that stop-and-frisk was unconstitutional and that the police must have a reasonable suspicion that a crime has been, is being, or is about to be committed by the suspect. The stop-and-frisk policy officially ended in January 2014.

"In my opinion, and this is not the police department saying this," Captain Strong said. "For all of its negatives, the stop-and-frisk policy, where officers were stopping people and checking for weapons, inhibited people from carrying guns illegally. I'm not getting into its constitutionality, but it reduced the number. Stop-and-frisk started as a good thing. It became overused, controls had to be implemented, and now we've overcompensated. People have become more brazen about carrying firearms. That inhibition helped prevent some violence. If I couldn't just walk around with a gun, then I had to be angry enough to go get my gun. You had to be stupid enough to still be here when I got back, and then I had to not think better of it during all that time."

"So how did stop-and-frisk become overused?" I asked as we walked to the other side of the floor.

"If you're being proactive, stopping people who are

carrying guns, then people stop carrying guns. Then it becomes self-defeating. If people aren't carrying guns anymore and you're still stopping people without guns, then what you're doing is wrong. It became a more significant problem, and where we really went wrong was when the number of stops became the driver of police activity. If you had five stop-and-frisks last week, this week the brass wanted six or seven. But there's only a finite number of bad guys, right? So, either you're stopping the same guys fifty times, or you're stopping everybody."

We entered an area where the lights were very dim, almost dark. "What's going on here?" I asked, waiting for my eyes to adjust.

"This is where we analyze bullets and casings from crime scenes. It's dark so that the analysts can see through their microscopes. Back here, they take the evidence from the street and try to link it to each other or link it to guns."

Captain Strong introduced me to a man standing over a microscope, Detective Rob Bustamante, a seventeen-year police veteran who had been doing firearms analysis for ten years. We shook hands, and Detective Bustamante explained what he was doing. "Ballistic evidence is recovered from a crime scene. It could be casings, bullets, and fragments. That evidence gets brought back here to the lab. We enter those casings and the marks on them into a database. The techs take ballistic images and collate the information with other regions around the country to see if these crime scenes link to other crimes in the past. We also provide expert testimony in court."

"And that's all part of the training in this division," Captain Strong added. "Testimony training, in addition to the operability training, which is six to ten months, is an additional eighteen months of training."

THE CRIME LAB, PART ONE—GUNS

I used my math skills. "So, in order to do this, you train for two years."

"Yes," said Bustamante, "and there's always continuous training."

"You're a valuable commodity," I responded. "They can't let you retire."

"Bustamante's one of the few people we have left," Captain Strong said, placing his hand on Bustamante's shoulder. "When the riots started and COVID and everything else, we lost more than half the unit."

Detective Bustamante nodded. "We lost a lot of experience," he agreed. "Thirty people."

My thinking went back to the recurring question of retention. "I need to ask you the magic question, which I ask everywhere I go," I said. "Are you understaffed or staffed where you want to be?" I had a feeling I already knew the answer.

"We have been understaffed for the last three years," Strong answered. "We are just now getting to the point where we've rebuilt."

> It seemed like recruitment and retention had become synonymous with rebuilding.

I'd heard the word "rebuild" a lot since I began asking this question. It seemed like recruitment and retention had become synonymous with rebuilding. "But doesn't rebuilding mean taking police officers from other places?"

"Yes," Strong said without hesitation. "We've had to take people off the street and spend years training them to be here at the lab. There was a point where we only had four examiners reviewing ballistic evidence for the entire city."

Detective Bustamante chimed in. "Last year, New York City had fifteen thousand pieces of ballistic evidence and four people to look at all of it."

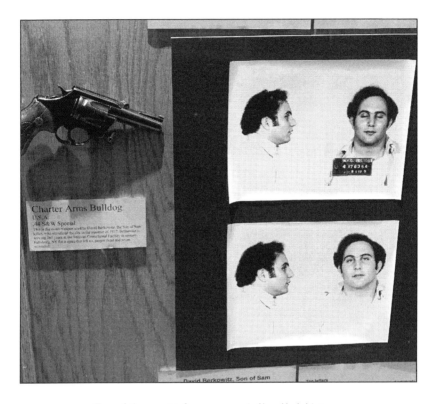

Two of the most infamous guns in New York history:
David Berkowitz's (above) and Mark David Chapman's (facing page).

Captain Strong had another section to show me, so I thanked Detective Bustamante for his time and knowledge. We went over to a bank of computers where, Captain Strong informed me, people were uploading information into a database that the NYPD shares at a national level through the ATF.

"Gun laws in New York are extremely tight. You can't buy guns in New York if you're not supposed to have a gun. But a gun that's bought in Kansas can make its way here. Either it gets stolen, or it's resold multiple times at gun shows."

I knew that all types of guns are sold at gun shows, but I knew very little about guns in general. "Do you have examples of the different kinds of firearms?"

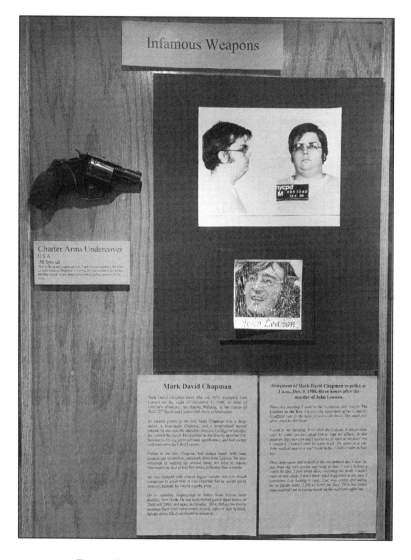

The gun Mark David Chapman used to kill John Lennon.

"Oh, yeah. Come this way."

The captain led me to another enormous file room with sliding bookcases. Instead of books, there was row after row of guns, gun parts, and ammunition magazines, sorted by caliber and manufacturer, going back to the early twentieth century. In addition to modern guns and antique guns, there was an entire collection of World War II weapons—American, Japanese, and German. This room served as a museum of firearms.

"All of these were either confiscated or surrendered," Captain Strong explained as I admired the stunning collection.

"Are guns the biggest issue for this lab?" I asked as we made our way to the elevator for the rest of my tour.

"I would say it's between guns and drugs," Captain Strong replied, hitting the "up" button.

Guns and drugs—the biggest death-dealers in New York City.

CHAPTER 13

The Crime Lab • *Part Two—Drugs*

*The first duty of man is the seeking after
and the investigation of truth.*

—Marcus Tullius Cicero, Roman Statesman

As we rode up to the fifth floor of the five-story building, Captain Strong and I talked about personal possession: individuals holding drugs but not selling.

"Personal possession cases are kind of a thing of the past," he said.

It shouldn't have surprised me, but the fact that the police didn't bust people for personal possession anymore still gives me pause. While some policies, like stop-and-frisk, have ended because of constitutionality issues, some drug laws, like possession of marijuana, have been reformed. And even when a law is still on the books for other drugs, I recalled learning from my ride-alongs that cops prioritize criminal activity and which ones to make arrests for, and then I was less surprised.

Captain Strong pointed out the Evidence Control Room, which was locked when we arrived. Although he could have entered, I was not allowed inside. Using the hallway, he showed me how deep the room was. It was long. "It's just shelves and shelves of every drug in the world," he said, with a mix of awe and sadness.

I wanted to know what they do in this lab. "When drugs are confiscated, they come here to be evaluated?"

"They do come here to be evaluated," Captain Strong said, "and it used to be that everything that was seized would come here to be tested. But with a marijuana case, even though those cases aren't being prosecuted, the police still confiscate the marijuana."

I remembered the police at the Three-Two, taking the crack away from the older gentleman on the street but not arresting him. I followed Captain Strong down the hall to another room.

The Drug Lab looked like a science laboratory: test tubes, beakers, microscopes, and a lot of foreign-looking equipment that appeared way too scientific for a guy like me.

The Drug Lab looked like a science laboratory: test tubes, beakers, microscopes, and a lot of foreign-looking equipment that appeared way too scientific for a guy like me.

I followed the captain to several black countertops on which several gadgets rested.

"The people who work here," he explained, "open up the drugs at these stations. They put the samples into vials, and those samples get loaded into machines that do all the analysis. Then, the analyst reads the report that comes from the machine. It might identify cocaine or fentanyl or heroin."

"Do you need that report to make an arrest?" I asked, the word "fentanyl" ringing in my head. I already knew that fentanyl is thirty to fifty times more potent than heroin and that fentanyl is now the most common drug involved in overdose deaths.

"The arrest is for 'suspicion of.' Then the report confirms, and they get charged accordingly. But if the test comes back negative—let's say that trunkful of marijuana turns out to be oregano—the charges are vacated."

I nodded in response as I looked around at the workers. "How many people work in this area?"

"They have ninety people on this floor, almost all civilian drug chemists with degrees in chemistry and/or biology."

That seemed like a lot of busy people. "So, even though personal possession charges are nil, drug crimes are still relevant?" I asked, hoping to make sense of the layers of this topic.

"They're still relevant," Strong assured me, "but the hunt is now for high-level distribution rather than street-level users. The volume is still there. What's changing is, who are we prosecuting?"

"What's the biggest challenge here?" I asked, thinking I might know the answer.

Captain Strong confirmed my assumption: "Fentanyl has become the biggest problem for the chemists because there are all these analogs." (Analogs are sometimes called "me-too "drugs. They're similar to the original drug, but with subtle differences.) "There's carfentanil, and there's fluorobutyrfentanyl and others. Each one shows up differently on the machines, and the chemists have to keep track of all the new and different variants the manufacturers are coming out with."

I wondered what the lab had been working on lately, so I asked the captain about recent cases.

"The biggest case we've had lately," he answered, "was the overdose at the Bronx daycare center."

Like most New Yorkers, I had heard about the case. A daycare center in the Bronx was being used as a fentanyl mill, and several children were exposed to the drug. A one-year-old boy died from exposure, and three other children were hospitalized. The fentanyl was hidden under the floor in the children's nap area, and even particles in the air can cause tremendous harm.

Drugs are a sad business.

CSU

After the Drug Lab, we headed down to the first floor to visit the Crime Scene Unit (CSU). We've all seen people on TV in hazmat suits—these are "those" people. The area had big garage doors, with vans and trucks inside and out in the parking lot.

"This place," Captain Strong said, "is basically like a firehouse because all their work happens in the field. All the calls come through here, the dispatch center. Then, the techs gather up their gear and head out. CSU trucks have everything they need in them. They respond, collect fingerprints and evidence, take pictures, look at blood spattering, things like that."

Nicholas Grenier, a retired lab guy, now with CSU, joined us for this part of my tour.

"How many calls do you think the unit gets in a day?" I asked Grenier, who told me to call him Nick.

"On a busy day, all our teams might leave here by noon. We're usually pretty busy, but you came on a quiet day."

Wanting to learn more about what they do, I asked, "Have you helped crack any big cases lately?"

"We don't crack cases. But we may find key pieces of evidence that a detective might overlook," said Nick. "That's why they call us in, and we walk and search the scenes."

"How many people are on your teams?"

"We have eight people per squad. Right now, we have seven squads—fifty-seven people."

Nick suggested we go see "the truck." I learned on the way that all the members of the Crime Scene Unit are investigators—either detectives or officers on track to become detectives.

"Do you have to be a detective to work crime scenes?" I asked.

"We start off as cops, police officers," Nick replied. "Then there's eighteen months of training, and eventually, you need to be a detective."

"The truck" itself was a marvel. The outside looked like an ambulance, except for the words "POLICE CRIME SCENE UNIT" printed all over. We opened a sliding side door and a double door on the back, and inside I saw shelves and counters with boxes and evidence bags, scales, DNA swabs, gloves, tripods, cameras, evidence markers (those little numbered signs you see on TV), and crime scene tape.

"Everything we need to process a job," Nick explained.

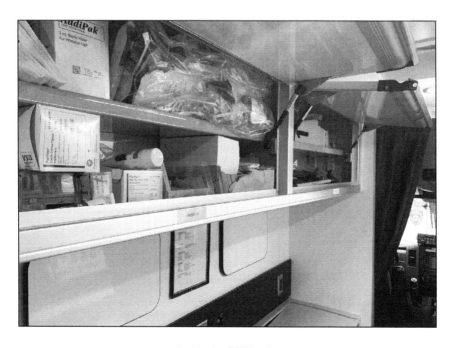

Inside the CSU Truck.

The item that impressed me the most was the Leica hand-held imaging laser scanner. I almost couldn't believe that an object that small could do what it does.

"What it does is it lets us capture data points at three-hundred-and-sixty degrees. That gives us a 'digital twin,' a three-dimensional image of the scene with exact measurements that we can refer back to at any time," Nick told me. "Let's say this all goes to court ten years down the line. Let's say they've leveled this building. We then have a 3D image rendering of exactly what the scene looked like ten years prior. You could walk a jury right through the scene."

The truck had so much equipment that every time Nick opened a cabinet, stuff fell out. "This is laser fog," he said, picking up a canister that had dropped to the floor. "We use this for ballistics. If you want to see bullet trajectories at night or in a dark room, you spray this stuff, and you can see the laser beams in a photograph to show where a shot came from. It's really cool stuff."

Nick went on to show me virtually everything else: gunshot residue swabs and luminol for showing latent blood in a scrubbed scene.

"Is there anything that really cleans blood that defeats your work?" I asked, thinking of all the movies I'd seen of criminals rubbing their fingerprints from doorknobs or scrubbing with bubbles to remove pools of blood from bathroom floors.

"Blood will seep into the floor, we find it," said Nick confidently. "You can't clean it well enough. You could repaint the house, and luminol will still show blood."

Thinking about all the other CSU stuff I'd seen on television, I asked about fingerprinting and DNA collection.

"It's sometimes hard to get a good print," Nick explained, "especially in cold weather. But DNA has come a long way. If your DNA is in the system, you're going to get caught."

THE CRIME LAB · PART TWO—DRUGS

"Do other cities across the country have this kind of crime scene van?" I asked as I hopped down from the van.

"I don't think most cities have as many as we do," he said, closing the back door, "but they do have these vans."

I left the lab thoroughly impressed with the equipment, the technology, and the people who know how to use it.

I had spent the day visiting the individual floors of the Crime Lab, each one with a large staff of highly skilled, trained, and intelligent people, both civilians and police officers, who work together to track down dangerous criminals using innovative technology. The Crime Lab is a vital connection between all the police units, from the precinct to the lab to the courthouse. When people talk about defunding the police, they don't realize that those funds pay for the Academy, the specialized divisions, and the labs that involve science in modern-day policing—all essential work that keeps us protected.

> When people talk about defunding the police, they don't realize that those funds pay for the Academy, the specialized divisions, and the labs that involve science in modern-day policing.

CHAPTER 14

The Courts · *Part One—The Judge*

Behind every ruling lies the power to inspire change.
—UNKNOWN

I don't think people understand the difficulties that go with urban policing. We think we understand because we see them in our neighborhoods or watch crime shows and the news. But only after riding with cops on the street and visiting the Academy and the Crime Lab was I beginning to develop some understanding. I needed to learn more and to reach out beyond the police department. I hadn't planned to go this far, but sometimes, the more you learn, the more questions you have.

What do other people who have regularly interacted with the police think? What do the people in the other part of the criminal justice system think of policing? Will their thoughts confirm what I had experienced, or would they give me a different perspective?

The law affects so many people in different ways, beginning with whether or not an officer makes an arrest, then how the lab conducts its survey of the scene, and then to the courts, who must decide the guilt and penalties of a crime. This all flows through a pipeline of legal intricacies, different lenses and experiences, and biases we can't fathom.

THE COURTS · PART ONE—THE JUDGE

I discovered that it's not so easy to get a sitting judge to go on the record with me. But a retired judge, with vast experience in the criminal justice system, was less difficult and possibly more informative.

I reached out to an eminent judge, who was kind enough to participate in an online Zoom meeting. Charles H. Solomon is a retired New York County Supreme Court justice. He retired in 2019 when he reached mandatory retirement age. Before he was appointed by New York City Mayor Ed Koch in 1986 to the New York City Criminal Court, Judge Solomon served as an assistant district attorney, prosecuting cases.

He was precisely punctual for our online meeting. I don't know if I expected to see wood-paneled bookcases behind him, but he sat in front of a plain beige wall so there were no distractions.

I asked him what he thought of community policing, the idea of the police integrating themselves into the community and partnering with citizens. I shared with him that community activists Big Russ Smith and Lisa Kenner had been very vocal about their support for this kind of policing.

Judge Solomon leaned in and said community policing is a great idea. "A cop on the beat going into all the stores introducing himself or herself, saying 'I'm here if you need me' or 'I'm going to be walking around this area' makes cops' presence known," he said. "It is a big deterrent to crime."

"What do you think the people in the communities want?" I asked.

"The law-abiding people say they want more police presence. Not everyone in public housing is a criminal. Most of them have families, they're raising kids, they have jobs, and they don't want crime in their buildings. These people are afraid to go in the elevators. They want cops around because the presence of a police officer in uniform is a big deterrent, no matter what anyone says."

I told him about my experience speaking with the community leaders in Manhattan and Brooklyn and how there didn't seem like there were enough police to go around to make outreach effective.

"There aren't," he agreed. "When [Mayor Rudolph] Giuliani was mayor in the nineties, there were almost forty thousand police officers. Now the count is down to less than thirty-four thousand."

"So how do we get back to safer streets?"

Judge Solomon paused before replying, "I don't know. No one has the real answer to this. That's the problem. Everyone's got opinions about what would be best, but there's no one answer that would be the right answer."

As a businessperson, I face challenges and problems all day long and pride myself on deep thinking to find a way around them. I couldn't help but see if our conversation could spark any solutions to consider. "You were on the bench for over thirty years and with the DA's office before and after," I said. "How do you think the nature of crime and police work have changed?"

The judge shifted his eyes thoughtfully, as if gathering a timeline from his memory. "Well, there was what was called the crack epidemic in the late eighties, and that increased the volume of indictments drastically," he said. "Half my caseload used to be narcotics sales, but that can expand or contract as the police want it to. They send out undercover officers, or they don't.

"But I think drugs are the real issue here because if you take away the drug element, the drug sales, crime is much more controllable. But you can't ignore the drugs. There are more people in the housing projects in gangs that sell drugs who control the projects, and everyone is afraid of them. Before crack, we didn't have these gangs selling drugs. Now we do, and the people who live in the projects are afraid. They're intimidated. These people want to raise their families, go to work, and want their kids to go to school, but their environment is crime-ridden."

From his tone and body language, I could tell that Judge Solomon was passionate about this topic and had talked with the citizens of these areas himself.

"Ask anyone who lives in the projects if they want more cops, fewer cops," he said, leaning in close to the camera, "every single one will say 'We want more cops.' Every single one."

> "Who'd want to be a police officer in New York City today? You'd have to have your head examined! You touch someone, and you get sued. You get spit on, and no one's going to back you up."

I mentioned the problem I was witnessing, that police departments everywhere had big problems with recruitment and retention.

Judge Solomon responded, "Who'd want to be a police officer in New York City today? You'd have to have your head examined! You touch someone, and you get sued. You get spit on, and no one's going to back you up. You know that."

"Yes," I answered, "I've seen it. I've been spending a lot of hours on the street, sir, and I'm trying to understand it all. I haven't spent time in the courtroom, but I'm sure it's frustrating with what to do with people who have ten or fifteen arrests, and they keep coming back to judges like you."

"It's more like people with fifteen felony convictions!"

Judge Solomon corrected. "Fifteen arrests, that's nothing. I've had people with over a hundred arrests."

And this was before the laws got more lenient on some crimes. I couldn't imagine what active judges see today.

I asked Judge Solomon what the number one problem was that he saw, and what he thought was the number one thing we could actually do, either for the community or the police department.

Judge Solomon thought for a moment, and said, "The main thing, I think, is change what people see every day. You walk into Duane Reade, and you want to buy soap, but it's locked up. I was on Lexington Avenue a few months ago. A guy gets out of a truck on the passenger side; it's a red light. The guy gets out and takes a piss in the middle of Lexington Avenue, three o'clock in the afternoon, without any regard for anything. You can't have that—you cannot. Because the people who see this stuff feel like crime is rampant, the law has broken down, and there's no security."

I understood what he meant, and mentioning quality of life reminded me of some of the conversations about the broken windows theory I had on the ride-alongs. "I was on two different ride-alongs, sir," I said. "On one, the cops let public defecation go. On the other, they stopped the guy and gave him a summons. But I wonder, you give the guy a summons, and what happens then?"

"Right!" Judge Solomon answered. "He's probably not going to show up [to court], not going to pay a fine. People aren't going to pay a fine for that or for jumping a turnstile on the subway. They just don't show up. They used to give out what were called *desk appearance tickets*. They used to call them *disappearance tickets* because the person didn't show up! Over fifty percent of those appearance tickets became warrants for arrest. I don't know the answer," he continued. "If you ask ten different judges their opinion, you're going to get seven different answers."

"I'm interested in your answer, sir."

"My answer is to have more police presence on the street. Walking the beat, walking around, getting to know the neighbors, getting to know the stores, getting to know the people, getting to know the criminals, who they are. You need that in neighborhoods. But they're drastically short-staffed." His answer echoed with answers I'd received from police and civilians alike.

Judge Solomon had mentioned repeat offenders, and I wanted to learn more. "What can you do with the people who've been arrested multiple times?"

"The only thing you can do is, if they have a drug problem, try to get some treatment for them. If they have mental health problems, try to get treatment for them. But people don't want to spend tax money on mental health treatment."

As I'd heard so many times from so many people, treatment would solve a lot of problems if there was adequate funding.

The Bottom Line

I still wanted to know what Judge Solomon had observed during his career as a judge that helped him come to conclusions about the nature of crime and policing, so I asked him what the biggest issue was during his time on the bench. "Any common denominators that point to a pervasive issue?" I asked.

"The recidivism," he answered without hesitation. (*Recidivism* is defined as the tendency of a convicted criminal to reoffend.) "I've had defendants in front of me, and then I get their kids in front of me twenty years later. It's like a family business. You put people in jail, they come out and commit more crimes.

Jail doesn't rehabilitate people; it makes them better criminals because, in jail, they associate with criminals. Think about it: you can't get a job if you're a convicted felon. Who's going to hire you? So, what do they do? Crime."

"Is it fixable?" I asked. "If you were in charge of the criminal justice system, could you fix it? Can you do something to change it, or is it too far gone?"

"We can do things, but *fixable* is a different question," the judge said. "We can do a lot to improve it. I think that the prisons could do more to provide education. Not just getting a GED, but learning how to live in society too."

Judge Solomon understands that the criminal life is, by definition, antisocial. He talked about programs that would benefit prisoners and prepare them for a life that wasn't antisocial.

"Jail doesn't rehabilitate people; it makes them better criminals because, in jail, they associate with criminals."

"You know, one little thing: everyone loves animals. Bring them into the jails; let inmates work with animals. Let them grow some compassion."

He was referring to expanding the Puppies Behind Bars program, where inmates are given eight-week-old puppies and taught to train them to become service dogs for the disabled. The puppies and prisoners are together twenty-four hours a day.

Judge Solomon continued, "Let them work in gardens, growing stuff. You'd be surprised what a lot of people in prison would really like to do. Teach them to be good cooks. Help them to develop skills instead of just letting them lift weights and play basketball all day. Most corrections officers and other employees of the correctional system that I've met say, 'I want to kiss my family in the morning and come home at night. I don't want problems. Let them [inmates] do whatever they want.' The officers don't want riots, and they don't want to be assaulted. They're not interested in rehabilitating these prisoners. Of course, some people are, but most just want safety in the jails and prisons." I thought about the idea of training programs in jails and prisons. It made sense to me.

I asked Judge Solomon what he thought his most significant accomplishment as a judge was. Having heard about his reputation as a tough judge, his answer surprised me.

"I gave kids a chance," he said. "You've got sixteen-, seventeen-, eighteen-year-old kids who do something stupid, or they hang around with the wrong people. I didn't want to put them in jail, and I told them I would give them a chance. You know, stay out of trouble, go to school, come back every couple of months in front of me; I want to make sure you're doing what you're supposed to be doing. I think it helped a lot of kids. Whereas other judges might not have, and I gave them three or four chances sometimes, you know, if they screwed up and had some weed on them or something."

"Looking back, do you think second chances was a good choice?"

"Oh, absolutely," he said and then paused. "However, I got burned very badly in one case, a case that really sticks in my mind. New Year's Eve, this kid was on Ninety-Ninth Street and First Avenue. Cops are coming from the New Year's Eve detail, coming up the avenue in an Emergency Services truck. This kid is in the middle of First Avenue, beating the crap out of somebody. So, the cops put their lights and siren on, and they get out of their vehicle. Two young cops, strong, fast, chase him. He throws a gun away. They get the gun, they get him. His father puts up forty thousand dollars' bail, which is considerable bail, and he's out, then he's appearing in court. The kid had a couple of minor arrests—one for a dice game or something, nothing serious. I was this far away from revoking, remanding him, giving the bail money back, and holding him in jail until he went to trial on the gun charge. But I didn't. I gave him a chance."

The judge paused momentarily, and I waited for him to continue.

"I read his name in the paper a couple of weeks later. He had killed somebody. That was on *my* watch. It got to me. I could have saved someone's life. A random killing, a kid on the playground, who was caught in the line of fire. I remember the deceased child's father making his victim impact statement on the day of sentencing. Everyone in the courtroom was crying. And I could have put that guy in jail."

I learned a lot from this tough yet compassionate judge: treatment as an alternative to incarceration, training inmates to become skilled and socialized, and that even with the best intentions, everyone make mistakes.

CHAPTER 15

The Courts • *Part Two—The Public Defender*

We educated, privileged lawyers have a professional and moral duty to represent the underrepresented in our society, to ensure that justice exists for all, both legal and economic justice.

—Supreme Court Justice Sonia Sotomayor[10]

Public defenders are another part of the criminal justice system. District attorneys prosecute, judges judge, and defense attorneys defend. Public defenders are employed by the government (either federal, state, county, or local) to defend those who cannot afford to hire private lawyers. Many public defenders are as dedicated and tenacious as any private defense attorney.

Dina Denlea is a public defender and chief of the County Court Division of the Legal Aid Society of Westchester County. Westchester County is just north of the Bronx. She has been an attorney in the criminal justice system for forty years. Most of

---

10 ABC News, "Sonia Sotomayor: A Look at Obama's Supreme Court Pick," May 26, 2009, https://abcnews.go.com/Politics/SoniaSotomayor/story?id=7676754&page=1.

her career has been spent on the other side of the aisle from the prosecutors, defending those who have been arrested by police.

I wanted to meet her because she is a smart and vigorous defender of individuals who are accused of crimes, and I needed to meet someone who might be able to add balance to the perspective I'd been developing.

Two days after meeting with Judge Solomon, I met with Ms. Denlea on Zoom, each of us in our respective office. My first question was a general one: I asked her if she had noticed a change over the course of her career in the way cops act and react toward people accused of crimes.

"Well, since the sixties and seventies, I think yes, a grand change," she replied, "but not tremendously on an individual basis that I've been seeing in my forty years of doing this."

I asked her what the Legal Aid Society of Westchester County was about—their mission, and what they did day to day.

"So we, the Legal Aid Society, by definition, represent the poor, the indigent. We have fifty-two local courts—Yonkers and Mount Vernon border New York City—and generate the largest number of cases. Yonkers in Westchester County is our largest court and probably generates about fifty-five percent of our caseload. It's a large city."

Because she defends people's due process rights, among other human rights, I wondered if she thought the police abused their position of authority and if she'd seen that kind of behavior. Before I could ask the question, she spoke.

"I'm not a police hater, just so you know," she said. "I'm not one of those folks that's anti-police. I believe they're here to protect us. I know many wonderful, dedicated police officers that I hold in very high regard. I don't think you can paint them with the same brushstroke. But there is exhaustion, I think, on the side of the police. They've got so much more on their plate these days. And I think there's exhaustion on the side of my clients and the community, where they think the police don't really care about them."

I thought it was interesting that she used the word "exhaustion" instead of "frustration," but the more I thought about it, I guess people on every side are just worn out by a system that doesn't work well for anybody.

Denlea continued, "I've seen cops who aren't concerned about the constitutional protections that we have; they're just not. They think, *This is a criminal, so I'm going to do what I have to do to get a conviction, and I'm going to protect myself by turning off the body cam videos and won't record what we should be recording.* That stuff still goes on."

We talked briefly about community outrage in the wake of the George Floyd murder on May 25, 2020, and the demonstrations that followed, and some of the reactionary responses in the federal government.

"Some of the political stuff has wreaked havoc on the criminal justice system," Ms. Denlea said.

I asked if she was referring to certain elements trying to demonize people of color or describing immigrants as criminals.

She nodded yes and continued, "And I think there's a huge need for the defense bar to stay engaged even when the going gets tough because we provide checks and balances. We get exhausted too, but without us trying to keep people honest in the way we pursue justice, it would be total havoc; it would just be mayhem. It would be people in control who aren't doing the right thing. So, there's a reason why we all exist, on both sides of the aisle. It's to keep the system as fair, honest, and as equitable as we can. That's why I do what I do."

I knew that Ms. Denlea had been admitted to the bar a few

years before the height of the crack epidemic in the eighties, so I asked her about the evolution of crime over time. "Then to now, what are the major causes of crime that you see, and where do you see your clients coming from?"

Ms. Denlea took off her glasses, leaned in toward the camera, and said, "The drug of choice has changed over the years, but drugs are the biggest problem. Fentanyl, as you know, is gigantic right now. Heroin had taken a backseat for many years, where we weren't seeing very much heroin. Now, there's a bit of a resurgence, and fentanyl is all over the place, which is pathetic."

"The drug of choice has changed over the years, but drugs are the biggest problem."

I shared what I had learned at the Crime Lab in Queens, discussing how much fentanyl is housed there and how shocking it was to see this becoming the drug of choice.

"I think it comes from despair," she said, explaining that many of her cases had been for defending people who'd been arrested for dealing. "Some of our clients start out by doing drugs to self-medicate for the horrors that they live in the lives that they have. Then, to support their habits, they have to sell. And then that obviously goes to stealing and other crimes to support those habits."

"Is treatment for addiction readily available for people who need it?"

"Since the pandemic, a lot of programs have closed down," she explained. "It's all economics and education. I'm a former teacher from a family of teachers, and I think the education system needs to step up and do more to keep kids in school because many of our clients have dropped out of school in ninth and tenth grade. They're on the streets. They don't have any way to earn a living. And when someone dangles a thousand dollars a week to work for one of the dealers compared to making minimum wage at Costco…" She held her palms out, as if to say, "What can you expect?"

I nodded my understanding.

"I believe a lot of our clients truly want to do the right thing," she said. "The odds are so stacked against them. So, when you have a kid with learning disabilities who doesn't have a family because of the myriad stories you hear about parents, et cetera, they're reared by grandparents or an uncle or an older brother. They have no diploma, no GED. So, they're driving for DoorDash, a job they can get. And often, they can't hold jobs for one reason or another. It's just the same cycle you see, generation after generation, decade after decade, until there's some intervention where you can pull those people out who have promise and a future."

Her observations reminded me of the recidivism Judge Solomon discussed during our Zoom meeting of a few days before, how crime turns into a "family business." I also thought about the young kids I saw in my ride-alongs, hanging out on gang-dominated street corners. "Is the court system equipped to help the cycle end?" I asked. "How would that happen?"

Ms. Denlea sat back and looked away from her screen as she composed an answer. "Some social service programs are out there, but they're all backed up," she said, with typical New York bluntness, edged with a lawyer's caution. "I'm sure the system helps people on some level, but not in a way that I think helps huge or significant numbers of people. Some programs try to help people find jobs. In Yonkers, Greyston Bakery has been hiring our clients since the early eighties."

Greyston Bakery was founded by Zen Master Bernie

Glassman (1939–2018) to employ individuals who face barriers to employment. Their process is called open hiring: they "accept anyone with a will to work," without interviews, background checks, or résumés. They also make the brownies that go into Ben & Jerry's ice cream.

"Greyston hires people even with felony convictions," Ms. Denlea continued. "There's another impediment in the process, right? Even if you have a certificate or training, will most companies hire someone with two prior felony convictions or someone with no felony convictions?"

"I see your point," I said, adding that Judge Solomon had mentioned the issue of employability in our conversation. "Earlier, you implied that sometimes police cut corners in how they operate. Are there safeguards in the process to keep police accountable? What about bodycams?"

"They can turn them on, and they can turn them off," she said. "I can't tell you how many times I've been able to see what was going on, but I can't hear, so I ask the district attorney, 'What happened?' and they say, "Oh, they forgot to turn the audio on, or for some reason, the audio wasn't working. Or in an interrogation room, the camera is right there, but suddenly you see them talking, but you can't hear a thing. What value does that provide to the defense? So, there's still some gamesmanship."

"But isn't there gamesmanship on both sides?" I asked. "For example, the complaints against police officers that are unsubstantiated, that don't hold up?"

"Well, if you're out in the field and a client is getting his ass kicked, and he's being mistreated by an officer, and there are three or four other officers present, that client then makes a complaint to the grievance committee. Who are the witnesses to the officer's behavior? Other police officers," Ms. Denlea said, her years of firsthand experience reflective in her authoritative tone. "So, a significant amount of those cases get thrown out all the time unless we have somebody from the third-floor window of an apartment house videotaping it on their cellular phone. That's one thing that does help us in those kinds of situations: another witness watching what's going on and videotaping it.

"Are some complaints exaggerated? I'm sure they are. Are some extremely valid? Yes, they are. And are they acted upon? No, not unless you have somebody with broken bones who lands in the hospital from a beating. Our Mount Vernon Police Department has been under investigation for many years by federal agencies because they have had more accusations than any of our other police departments."

I didn't expect to hear that. Sometimes, during the process of researching this book, something or someone made me realize I'd been living in a bubble all these years, which prompted another question. "In New York City, proper mental health support seems to be almost nonexistent compared to forty years ago. What about Westchester?" I asked. "Is there some support in place for a homeless guy who hit someone with a brick because the voices in his head told him to? Is there someplace for him to go?"

"I'm hugely concerned about mentally infirm people," Ms. Denlea said. "We have a specialized Mental Health Court in Westchester County. Our administrative judge, Anne Minihan, supervises that court, and it's a very strict program that deals with people with mental health issues who get in trouble with the law and are nonviolent. It does exceedingly well with some folks, but there are limitations. You have to live in Westchester County. Also, it rarely takes violent crimes.

"But we have crimes on the books that are called violent crimes when there is no violence intended, like burglary in the second degree. If someone goes up on your porch at eleven o'clock in the morning, opens your door, walks in, and steals food out of your kitchen, that's a burglary in the second degree, considered a violent crime. So they would not be eligible for mental health court."

I'd seen quite a few people on the streets during my ride-alongs who probably suffered from some form of mental illness; some were pointed out by police officers who knew them. "Has the occurrence of crime by people with mental health problems increased?" I asked.

"Yes," she said emphatically, "the number of those cases has increased. It breaks my heart. Nobody wakes up in the morning and says, 'Yay, another day where I'm bipolar and schizophrenic and have nothing to eat and nowhere to live.' We don't have as many shelters as we used to have. Near my office in White Plains, you see homeless people all over. You see them talking to themselves on the sidewalks, panhandling for money. We should have more programs. There used to be residential programs. Now, I think there are three of them in the whole county."

> I'd seen quite a few people on the streets during my ride-alongs who probably suffered from some form of mental illness.

I wanted to get back to the topic of bridging the gap between community and police. I was curious about how that looked in Westchester County as opposed to New York City. "In some parts of New York City," I said, "the public seems to see the police as an occupying force rather than a partner. Does that also happen in parts of Westchester?"

"Well, we're so diverse. In places like Scarsdale and Bedford, they're a little more community-based. The high schools would have programs asking lawyers, prosecutors, defense attorneys, and judges to speak to the students."

I know these areas well, since I've lived in that area for a lot of my adult life. "Those are kind of privileged towns," I pointed out.

"Exactly. This brings us back to what I was saying about Mount Vernon and Yonkers. Are we reaching Michael on Ashburn Avenue in Yonkers, who gets up in the morning and has to step over fifteen junkies in order to get to school? The cards are against him. Kudos to the D.A.; they're required to speak at schools and nursing homes and community organizations, so they're trying to get into the communities. But there's a certain naivete when politicians think they're educating people without meeting them at their level.

"I think the kid in Yonkers is a gang member because he has to be because he has no other support, and he looks for familiarity and group connection. He's not avoiding buying that gun or possessing that gun because there's a billboard telling him he can do three-and-a-half years in prison."

Dina Denlea opened my eyes to a lot of what was going on in an area close to me. Between Syracuse and Westchester County, I discovered that the same problems exist pretty much everywhere. Ms. Denlea and Judge Solomon convinced me that the legal system is doing its best to keep up, but it could be doing better.

CHAPTER 16

Underground · *The Times Square Subway Hub*

*Just because you don't see something
doesn't mean it isn't there.*

—R. C. Lewis, SPINNING STARLIGHT[11]

I wanted to go back into New York City to see what I hadn't yet seen. I thought of a few places, but one hit me as most significant. There's an old song that goes, "The people ride in a hole in the ground." Back in my youth, I rode the subway daily, before I got my driver's license. What kind of policing goes on in the New York Subway system and its center, Times Square?

Times Square station entrance to the New York City subway system.

---

11 R. C. Lewis, *Spinning Starlight* (Little, Brown Books for Young Readers, 2015), [page #].

The NYC Subway system was policed by the Transit Police Department from 1949 to 1995 when then-Mayor Rudy Giuliani fully incorporated the department back into the NYPD, at which point the Transit Police Department was renamed the Transit Bureau.

Times Square is, in many ways, the heart of New York City, and the twelve subway lines that feed into and out of Times Square are what keep the city flowing. The Times Square–42nd Street station is a major New York City Subway station complex located under Times Square, at the intersection of 42nd Street, Seventh Avenue, and Broadway, in Midtown Manhattan.

Even if you've been to the subway complex under Times Square, you may not have an idea of its vastness. It warrants its own police station, the Transit Bureau Manhattan Task Force, located at 685 Eighth Avenue, where I met with the task force commanding officer, Captain Tamecca Greene, who has been a police officer since 2006 and rose to the rank of captain in 2023. Since we met, Captain Greene is now the Captain of Transit Bureau District 32.

A task force is a subunit within a district, in this case, Transit District 1. So even though it's called the Transit Bureau Manhattan Task Force, the task force is specific to the Times Square underground complex.

Compared to most of the NYC Subway system, the Times Square station is an anomaly. Unlike many other stations, it's well-managed, appropriately staffed, and well-policed. As the main hub, it has to be—otherwise, the whole city would be affected.

There are twenty-six entrances to the station, plus one exit-only opening. There are sixty-one officers assigned to the Times Square transit complex. That's just underground; that number doesn't even include the streets of Times Square, policed by a different task force. The police who work out of 685 Eighth

Avenue cover eight different platforms with twelve different train lines running through.

Captain Tamecca Greene

"The most difficult part of managing the Times Square task force," Captain Greene told me, "are all the *fly-ins*, all the officers that are not assigned to the task force that come to Times Square to help us out. If you get different people every day, it's a little harder to train them, to get them to see the vision that you have for Times Square. It's like getting a different substitute teacher every day. That's ten to twenty-two people a day."

The Metropolitan Transportation Authority (MTA) reported in 2023 that the Times Square–42nd Street complex, including the Eighth Avenue Line, is the busiest station complex in the system, serving 65,020,294 passengers in 2019. They come from everywhere—commuters from all five boroughs, tourists, and workers from out of town and outside the country. The Times Square complex connects to the Port Authority Bus Terminal and a shuttle to Grand Central Station on the East Side of Manhattan.

"And everybody's moving," Captain Greene said.

There have been a significant number of violent crimes that made national news that have happened in the subway system of New York City, including the boroughs. I asked Captain Greene for an opinion: "Is it getting worse, or are isolated incidents getting too much attention in the media?"

> "If you think about how many people we have going through the transit system every day, the number of incidents is minuscule."

"Isolated cases get lots of media attention, for sure. If you think about how many people we have going through the transit system every day, the number of incidents is minuscule. Not only that, if you look at the numbers, you'll see that crime has decreased dramatically."

I noted that although the number of incidents is statistically tiny, every violent incident means someone gets hurt or threatened. In 2024, a billion people rode the NYC Subway. If one one-thousandth of one percent of subway riders is involved in a violent incident, that's 100,000 people in one year. Still, the police are doing the best that they can.

"In the Times Square complex alone," Captain Green said, "we've had a ninety percent decrease in subway crime compared to a year ago."

"Why do you think that is?" I asked.

"We came in in early in 2023, did a proper crime analysis, and changed some things around," she said. "Before I became captain, we used to have officers fixed, where they would stay in one place. But with our resources so limited, I had to figure out how to make it look like we have more officers than we actually have. So, I made them move. Instead of having them stationary, where only people passing will see them, they walk the platform from the north end to the south end, and if people see the same two cops five times, they think they've seen ten cops. We get more coverage, more visibility."

The captain told me that grand larcenies comprised most of the crime reported in the station in 2022 to 2023. In New York, *grand larceny* is defined as "wrongfully taking, withholding, or obtaining property from its rightful owner, with the aim to either take the property for themselves or someone else or to deprive the rightful owner of said property."

"We put together a grand larceny initiative, and now grand larceny is not the leading crime."

The initiative, Captain Greene told me, involved utilizing between ten and thirty uniformed volunteer auxiliary police to educate commuters on how to keep themselves safe. These auxiliary civilian officers also added to the police presence in the Times Square station.

"What is the leading crime now?" I asked, unsure if I wanted to hear the answer.

"Assault Two," she said casually, as we walked past a sign for the 1, 2, and 3 trains.

According to the New York Penal Law, "A person is guilty of assault in the second degree when, with intent to cause serious physical injury to another person, he causes such injury to such person or to a third person."

The way Captain Greene defined it was, "Unprovoked assault. One person attacking another person. A punch in the face, a stabbing. But again, we've had seven incidents this year; last year, we had thirty-four. What we're doing is working. And we have cameras pretty much everywhere." Captain Greene showed me monitors of cameras focused on turnstiles at a particular exit.

"Do people still jump turnstiles?" I asked.

"Absolutely! So many jumpers!" Captain Greene said. "Believe it or not, it's the people who are jumping who are committing the crimes. Ninety percent of the people who commit crimes in transit also don't pay their fare."

Remembering so many of my discussions with police about prioritizing which offenses to respond to in order to prioritize, I asked the captain, "So what do you do?"

"We address everything we see. Now, addressing doesn't always mean enforcing," she said, as we stood not too far from a row of turnstiles. "It means you are being stopped because you committed a violation. We check you for wants and warrants; if you don't have a history, maybe I'll give you a break. But if you've got a history, especially of crimes in transit, then you're going to be arrested."

I asked if she thought the word had gotten out on the street not to mess around in the Times Square station. Captain Greene agreed that that might be one reason for their success.

I asked how officers are assigned to the Task Force, and Captain Greene told me that when she was promoted to the position, she was given a team that had just completed field training. Field training is post-Academy "rookie" training in the field. After field training, officers are assigned where needed, including transit. Additionally, officers can request assignments.

Given the number of people passing through the station every day, I was curious about acts of terrorism. I wanted to know how prepared they might be for that kind of disaster—bombings or gassings—especially in light of fewer cops we had patrolling the stations.

"In 2017, a guy detonated a homemade bomb in one of the passageways down here. The only person injured in that case was the bomber himself. We had to evacuate, which is very hard to do with trains full of people. So, first, we had to contact the MTA and stop all train service to this station. We shut this station down for a half hour. But that affects the entire city. Once counterterrorism got involved and we knew what was happening, trains could move again, bypassing this station."

I could hardly imagine that kind of disruption. "So, there's a process in place for dealing with terror incidents?"

"Absolutely. About a month or two ago, something happened topside," Greene continued, referring to the streets above us, "where a grenade was found left in an Uber. As soon as we learned of it, we shut down the entire Seventh Avenue side, including the shuttle to Grand Central, and pushed everyone to Eighth Avenue because my job is to keep everyone safe underground. Once they were cleared upstairs, we could resume service here."

As a lifelong New Yorker who prided himself on navigating this underground world, I was astounded to learn how much goes on that we never see. In fact, I knew if I polled a hundred New Yorkers, none of them would realize the amount of police attention and energy going on underground.

CHAPTER 17

Managing the Masses •
The Strategic Response Group's Crowd Management Unit

Crowds are somewhat like the sphinx of ancient fable: It is necessary to arrive at a solution of the problems offered by their psychology or to resign ourselves to being devoured by them.

—GUSTAVE LE BON, THE CROWD:
A STUDY OF THE POPULAR MIND[12]

The NYPD's Strategic Response Group (SRG) is the unit that deals with counterterrorism and the policing of political protests. The SRG is composed of five borough-based units and the Crowd Management Unit, which also maintains a bicycle fleet. The SRG has, in the past, been heavily criticized for its use of force in crowd control situations. I wanted to see how they handled things in the real world today.

I was invited by SRG leadership to spend a chilly September day with SRG's Crowd Management Group. Outside United Nations Headquarters, I first met with Officer Thomas

---

12 Gustave Le Bon, *The Crowd: A Study of the Popular Mind* (Macmillan, 1896), 99.

Corcoran, who joined the Police Department in 2011 and has been with the Crowd Management Unit since 2019. The Crowd Management Unit is the part of the Strategic Response Group that supports the SRG's activities in the five boroughs with personnel and equipment.

Officer Thomas Corcoran

Corcoran told me that the Strategic Response Group has, in total, around 500 members.

This was the opening day of the United Nations General Assembly 2024, a pretty busy day for Officer Corcoran's unit, which handles huge gatherings supplemented by uniformed officers from the rest of the NYPD. It's a busy day every year, but this year, there would be a lot of protesters on both sides of the Israel/Hamas War.

"Throughout the city, there are a lot [of protests] that go on every single day that we monitor, and we respond to if we have to, depending on the size of the protest group," Officer Corcoran explained. "If the protesters need escorts, or if there's an arrest situation, we're there. Most of the time, we're just there to help people honor their First Amendment rights while allowing the rest of the people of the City of New York to travel freely."

"Does your group handle crowd control when the president comes into the city?"

"Yes, anytime POTUS comes in, or any high-profile visitor, we get dispatched."

I asked Corcoran about liaising with the Secret Service, and he said the Secret Service was there to protect the president, and his group was there to protect the people of New York City. They didn't cross paths much.

The 2024 student protests at Columbia University were also managed by the Crowd Management Unit. Pro-Palestinian students set up a fifty-tent encampment on the Columbia campus. "Was that a strain on your resources?"

"I wouldn't call it a strain," Officer Corcoran answered. "It's just part of the job. We're here to make sure everything goes smoothly for everybody."

While the Strategic Response Group has five borough-based units, the Crowd Management Unit is city-wide, providing its services as needed in every borough.

"If I wanted to organize a protest, do I need to do some kind of paperwork?"

"Yes," Corcoran answered. "You have to go down to City Hall and apply for a permit."

"Do most people do that?" I asked.

"The vast majority do. Sometimes someone will start a protest without a permit, but most people follow the rules."

Knowing how many large-crowd events go on in New York City on any given day, I felt the need to ask him if any events, like ball games or rock concerts, were particularly notable or enjoyable for him personally.

"One of my favorite times was the year I got to work the U.S. Open Tennis Tournament in Queens; that was a wonderful time."

I was surprised that they provide security for sporting events, although I've seen plenty of police presence at Yankee Stadium and Madison Square Garden during the many times I've been to both, for business and for pleasure.

I thought of the 2003 Springsteen concert when every cop at Shea Stadium turned their back on the stage when Springsteen sang "American Skin," a song about a well-known police shooting. But that was over twenty years ago. "What's an example of an event that didn't go so well?"

"I would have to say, most of 2020 was difficult."

I raised an eyebrow.

"Between the protests and COVID," Corcoran clarified, "it was an interesting year for everybody. Even with COVID, we all had to show up for work every day."

Officer Corcoran then introduced me to Captain David Miller, Commanding Officer of the Crowd Management Unit. Captain Miller joined the force in 1993. I asked him for an overview of what the unit does.

"We have a dual purpose," Miller replied. "My guys will train other officers in crowd management, public order, all the way up to crowd control. Methods and ideologies of protesters, how protesters act, understanding crowd psychology and the contagion of crowd behavior—explaining those things are the training aspect. Then we move into an operational role."

I asked him what concerns him most about the job of managing gigantic crowds in a place like New York City.

"I want to make sure everyone goes home safe. I never want to make the call to anyone and say, 'Your son, your daughter, may not be coming home tonight, is seriously hurt,' or worse. So, when I do training, I try to put their bodies and minds where they have never been. When they face a dangerous situation, they'll know how to react. We want to have the interaction ahead of time in a training environment that allows them to make mistakes where we can control it before they're in the streets.

"I want to make sure everyone goes home safe."

"We don't take officers straight out of the Academy," Captain Miller went on. "We take officers with three years or more. We look at their background, and once they're assigned to SRG, they get a six-week Academy-based training, strictly for our team."

That reminded me of some of the advanced training I saw at the Academy, notably the SCUBA team.

"Then the training continues with us. Our team has had bottles thrown at us, fireworks—you name it. We've practiced handling those situations before they happen."

I couldn't ignore the protests beginning around us. "What's your plan for today?" I asked.

Captain Miller's answer was immediate. "We're going to do crowd control. Based on the intelligence we've received, tonight's going to be a large-scale protest, with up to ten thousand people attempting to march through the streets. Potentially, there could be violence, bottle-throwing, things of that nature."

THE RIDE-ALONGS

The Crowd Management Unit Prepares for Protest

The NYPD liaises with the N.Y. Fire Department Bureau of Emergency Medical Services for big gatherings like today's protest. I spoke briefly with Fire Department Deputy Chief Gregg Brady, who told me that his Emergency Medical Services team stands by in case anyone, protester, police officer, or passerby, is injured or needs medical assistance.

While I still had him there, I asked Captain Miller, "What are you hoping to accomplish here?"

"We're looking to control and take out any agitators. We don't want to arrest ten thousand people; we have no problem with the First Amendment, but those who are agitating the crowd, we want to stop them before it becomes mob mentality. Some of the protest groups are pretty sophisticated, and they train each other," Miller said. "They know how to get large numbers of people; they communicate using encrypted messaging apps, but generally, they're not violent. My unit [Crowd Management] is only coming in if there's violence or the threat of violence. There may be counter-protests, two groups clashing; we'll step in."

The captain explained some of their crowd-management strategies, which I can't share here. Still, the amount of planning, logistics, equipment (from bicycles to drones), and psychology that goes into managing large groups of people is mind-blowing.

"This morning, there were protesters trying to block First Avenue," Miller told me. "We made thirty-one arrests, people that wouldn't move and were blocking the street."

"Where do you take people when you arrest them?" I asked. "Is that a thirty-one-person burden on a precinct?"

"No, we have MAP-C, the Mass Arrest Processing Center, downtown at One Police Plaza [NYPD Headquarters]. They go through an arrest process. Whether they're given a summons or a desk appearance ticket, or they're going before a judge, that's all based on the crime they've committed and what their past history is."

I asked Captain Miller what the most complicated time had been for his unit.

> The amount of planning, logistics, equipment (from bicycles to drones), and psychology that goes into managing large groups of people is mind-blowing.

"The most trying time was during the BLM [Black Lives Matter] protests in the summer of 2020. I look at that as a perfect storm. Here's how I see that year," Captain Miller said.

"March twelfth was the day the world shut down. Everything we could do before that day, suddenly we were all told, no, we can't. Women giving birth couldn't stay in the hospital. Graduations were going virtual. School, in general, went virtual. All the shared human experiences, we couldn't do."

Echoes of "essential" and "non-essential workers" rang through my head. "And you guys still had to go to work," I said.

"Yes, and we didn't know what was going to happen," he said, hearkening back to that time when these essential workers continued to serve despite being uncertain of how dangerous the virus was. "But the benefit of that summer was that we learned we could handle a lot more than we thought we could before. The Black Lives Matter protests put everything else in perspective."

As officers assembled formally around the perimeter, Officer Corcoran pointed out that his team was always on alert, especially with a high-profile event like the U.N. General Assembly. He described several security measures in place for large gatherings, but, again, I'm not able to share those proprietary details here.

Corcoran did say one last thing before he followed Captain Miller to their posts. I could hear the pride in his voice as he shook my hand and assured me, "We want to make sure that, whatever is going on, for most people, it's just a regular day in New York City."

CHAPTER 18

The Takedown · Full Circle with the Four-Six

We are the line ... the people who keep the people in this city safe.

—DEPUTY INSPECTOR CRAIG EDELMAN

I was back in the Fordham section of the Bronx, the 46th Precinct, where a notorious gang known as the Slattery Gang had been terrorizing the neighborhood. The Slattery Gang, also known as "Slaughtery" and "S-block," was responsible for over a dozen shootings, including several murders. Detectives had been investigating and building a case against twenty-two gang members, with an average age of twenty.

About two months before the July 31 takedown, Deputy Inspector Craig Edelman invited me to ride along, as the NYPD Gun Violence Suppression Division planned to send more than one hundred detectives to simultaneously raid twenty-two separate residences, all homes to members of the Slattery Gang. These individuals had already been thoroughly investigated by detectives and indicted by a single grand jury.

The more I learned about the planning of this operation, the more astonished I was. For one thing, Inspector Edelman said he wouldn't be able to tell me the date, time, and staging location until a day or two before the event. There was a chain of trust that couldn't be broken because if news of this plan got out, the integrity of the investigation would be compromised. This team had gone all out, from investigation to obtaining warrants to meticulous planning and timing, to ensure those arrested would be put in prison and not get out on the street again.

According to the Police Department, the NYPD Gun Violence Suppression Division "identifies individuals and organizations responsible for the trafficking and sale of illegal firearms in New York City and dismantles them." They do this using undercover police officers and confidential informants, and their goal is to reduce the number of guns on the streets. Gun sales and trafficking were among the criminal counts the Slattery Gang would be charged with. According to the NYPD website, the division also "organizes Violence Reduction Task Forces to target violent groups using firearms throughout the city."

This was going to be big for the city and for the Division, and I was excited to be part of it. I was also scared to death.

This was going to be big for the city and for the Division, and I was excited to be part of it. I was also scared to death.

It was pre-dawn, about 5 a.m., when I parked my car in a secured outdoor area known only to the NYPD, one local television reporter (and her cameraman), and me. I walked through the darkness into an open area made bright by floodlights and found myself standing in a circle of about one hundred detectives from all over the city, many of whom wore body armor. The scene reminded me of something out of a Batman movie.

Everyone was locked into one purpose: make twenty-two

simultaneous arrests without one gang member alerting anyone else. Such a synchronization required an almost telepathic level of concentration and communication.

There was energy in this group—a little tension, and a lot of focus and powerful pride in what they were there to do. Nobody kidded around; everybody was serious and alert, even at five in the morning. In the middle of the circle stood Detective Bureau Assistant Chief Jason Savino, commander of the Gun Violence Suppression Division. He wore a sharp blue suit and tie and addressed the team, "When I woke up this morning, the first thing I thought was, 'Damn, I love being a cop.' And you are the reason." He paced the circle so he could look the men and women surrounding him in the eye. "These cases are the single most impactful reason why shootings continue to trend down. Now, one shooting is too many, but shootings are down, and this crew is the reason why.

"Today, twenty-two individuals are going down. Nineteen of them are trigger-pullers—many more than once. We're talking shootings in broad daylight, school hours, we're talking shootings out of moving vehicles, off of scooters, and why? Because of drill rap."

I mentioned "drill rap" back in chapter 1: Drill rap is a subgenre of gangsta rap about shooting, killing, and revenge. Then there's a level of drill rap about disrespecting another gang member who got killed.

Assistant Chief Savino talked about a couple of recent incidents involving Slattery, one involving the murder of a fourteen-year-old boy, Prince Shabazz, ambushed along with his brother, and how the shooting was followed up with a series of drill raps, "adding insult to the crime, saying over and over 'Prince is dead, Prince is dead!'"

I could tell the group was familiar with the murder as their heads bowed while they continued soaking in Chief Savino's words. "As you take these individuals out of their residences and put them, quite frankly, where they belong, pay attention to the community. Because when you get those subtle nods and subtle smiles, you know that they know that they're safer as a result of your work."

Chief Savino was followed by Deputy Inspector Craig Edelman, who spoke about the yearlong work that had been done to justify and organize the takedown and the dangerous people they were about to arrest. "The work that was done on this case was so tremendous; the management and meticulousness that Detective Brandon Ravelo displayed—I don't think there's a perfect case, but this would be close to it. I couldn't be more impressed." He also publicly commended the work of Sergeant Chris Neil.

Locked and loaded, the cops were pepped and prepped. With their equipment assembled, they headed toward their cars and vans.

The officers had to be careful; many of these gang members lived with their families—parents, partners, children—any of whom could get hurt or who might be eligible for arrest, too. The officers needed tremendous foresight: *Who's at the exits? Who's on the roof? Who's hiding in a closet?* They needed to keep the innocent out of harm's way while swiftly capturing the allegedly guilty.

I got in an unmarked car with Detective Sergeant Alexander Rapp.

"The hope is," he told me, "that all these people are at their residences." (If one person wasn't, it could tip off the others who were on the raid list.) "All these people are in a gang together; they've committed violence together: shootings, homicides, robberies. They're all connected. And they've done just about all their violence in the Four-Six," Sergeant Rapp explained.

While he waited for the radio call to move out, Sergeant Rapp and I discussed the average age of the members of this gang, and of many others. How many were just kids? The prevalence of juvenile crime and gangs using underage kids to commit crimes is high. *Why?* I wondered.

"Criminals are smart," Rapp remarked. "If they can use a kid whose record is going to get wiped, the adult-age leaders stay clean."

I remembered my conversation with Judge Solomon about how he tried to give second and third chances to kids, so this approach on the gang leaders' part made sense.

The command to move came over the radio, and we rolled out, along with four or five other cars, to serve warrants.

> The prevalence of juvenile crime and gangs using underage kids to commit crimes is high.

We pulled over in front of an apartment building, and Rapp unbuckled and swung out of the car in one smooth move to serve a warrant. Arrests were going on all over the neighborhood, and I stayed in the car. My heart raced as I watched people being pulled out of their buildings in handcuffs and placed in a police van. There was one couple, both being arrested, in which the woman was eight months pregnant. I don't know if I was more fearful or sorrowful. Most of these arrests were within a block or two of the precinct station.

One headline-making arrest was of an eighteen-year-old female drill rapper and (alleged) gang leader.

As the gang member was being led away in handcuffs, the reporter asked her, "Are you a trigger puller?"

She answered, "The only thing I pull is your mother!"

And that was one of the politest things I heard these (alleged) gang members say.

As the sun got higher in the sky, the police collected weapons and gang members, one of whom was only sixteen.

I said to Sergeant Rapp, "It looks like not everyone was home, but you arrested twenty out of twenty-two people today. Most of them are going away for multiple years."

"We hope," he answered.

While it was still morning, Sergeant Rapp and I drove to the precinct and went downstairs to watch these young men and women get put in cells, and the hollering and threats were as scary as hell. Loud, blustering bravado and lots of cursing, yelling, and trash-talk filled the cell area—except for one kid asking for a phone call. He wanted to call his mother.

And with all the profanity and bluster, the officers stayed calm and professional. They didn't react, not even slightly. Occasionally, an officer would say under his breath, "You guys are going to jail." What else was there to say? Most of the gang members acted like this was an ordinary arrest, like they'd be out of the holding cells as soon as they could see a lawyer and be arraigned. They didn't realize they weren't going home anytime soon.

That day was a full-circle moment for me, back to the beginning—riding along in the Four-Six, not knowing what was going to happen—but what I saw that day went a lot deeper than patrolling.

Most days, cops do their job without a great sense of accomplishment. Nobody says, "Oh boy, we really defeated crime today." It can seem endless. But that day, the police had put a dent in crime and made a difference in their neighborhood.

"Are any of these individuals going to get out on bail?" I asked.

"It depends on the judge," Sergeant Rapp said, "and the

number of charges they have coming to them in addition to conspiracy."

"What exactly do you mean when you say *conspiracy*?"

"All these individuals conspired, as a gang, to commit these crimes," he explained. "All the shootings, all the robberies, all the individual crimes were set up as a group. If we did shootings in furtherance of our gang, that's a conspiracy."

That made it a RICO takedown, according to the Racketeer Influenced and Criminal Organizations Act. The RICO Act aims to dismantle entire criminal organizations, rather than just prosecuting individual members, and provides for federal charges and penalties in addition to local law.

I thought about how hard it must be to try to prove that a crime was committed to further a criminal enterprise. And establishing that proof must take many person-hours.

* * *

A week after the takedown, I spoke briefly with Inspector Edelman. Everyone was still in jail—either remanded or with such high bail that they weren't going anywhere.

> It's terrifying how a small number of people could put an entire community on edge.

It also struck me how much money is spent to build a case this grand. Detectives worked on putting this case together for a year. This day's operation alone involved a hundred law-enforcement personnel and tons of equipment, vehicles, and other resources, all to put away twenty young people with guns. Then, the expense of transporting, booking, jailing, and feeding, coupled with a trial for each of the young people including their defenders, and after that, the cost of imprisonment.

But beyond the taxpayers' pockets, I considered the gang's damage to the neighborhood—the danger and the fear they caused. It's terrifying how a small number of people could put an entire community on edge. And I thought about how the arrest of that gang was a big cloud lifted off the neighborhood, and this takedown was an accomplishment civilians and police together could be proud of.

And my next thought was a series of unanswered questions: *Which gang will step in and take over the territory?* There are five or six gangs in the Four-Six alone. *How do we take our city back? How does a community grow if it has to tolerate this kind of gun violence? How do families raise children safely in a place where thugs make thug life seem attractive to a kid?*

I'm still shaking my head.

CHAPTER 19

A Civilian's Conclusions · *My Two Cents*

Everything we hear is an opinion, not a fact.
Everything we see is a perspective, not the truth.

—Marcus Aurelius, Roman Emperor
and Stoic philosopher

I want to thank all the officers, sergeants, lieutenants, captains, people at the executive level, community leaders, and legal professionals who helped make this book possible. Thank you all for allowing me into your world.

I learned a lot doing the research, none of which involved a library or sitting at my computer. I had a grand adventure, met ordinary and extraordinary people, and had many of my questions answered. And I've drawn a few conclusions from what I've learned.

While writing this book, I kept asking myself the same thing I ask myself when I'm making a deal with the execs at Yankee Stadium, meeting with a championship team, or sitting in a room with Derek Jeter: *How the hell did I get here?*

It's because I'm persistent and somewhat fearless when I want to find something out. Then, the level of my curiosity supersedes my common sense, and I start asking questions and reaching out for answers.

I didn't write this book to try to change anyone's mind. I hope that I've provided an opportunity to see what most of us don't get to see and to think deeper and make up your own mind. Draw your own conclusions. Still, I have a few ideas of my own that I'd like to share with you.

The first thing I need to tell you: On every ride-along I did, there was never a moment where I thought, *I'm with police officers in the back of a police car. What could go wrong?* Not for a minute did I feel safe. Not once did I stop thinking about the things that could happen at any moment. Even wearing a bulletproof vest, in the company of the police, there was always a sense of danger and a wave of fear.

So I think about the citizens who live and work in these precincts, never knowing what might happen when they turn the next corner. I also think about the police officers who try to protect those citizens and keep them as safe as possible, despite the challenges lurking around them—and their own fear. Living in that fear sucks. And it's a shame.

I often say that common sense isn't common practice. I know there are many good reasons why necessary changes aren't being made, and it's relatively easy for me to sit in the back of a police car and make judgments. I recognize and realize that many of the steps that need to be taken are very hard to execute. But they're still needed. Here's my take:

As I mentioned earlier, crime is costly. It's terrible that crime even exists, but it does. Crime has been going on since Cain killed Abel—the first murder. So, we're not getting rid of all crime. My question is, can a percentage of crime be avoided?

It's apparent to me, and many others, that minor-league crime leads to major-league crime. In his book *The Profession:*

A Memoir of Community, Race, and the Arc of Policing in America, former Police Commissioner Bill Bratton, who led both the NYPD and the LAPD, wrote about the broken windows theory of policing. As explained earlier, this theory suggests that visible signs of crime create an environment that encourages more crime, and when police target minor crimes, like vandalism and turnstile-jumping, that creates an atmosphere of lawfulness. Do we go back to broken windows? Stop and frisk? Is there a better way?

As you think about the issues raised in this book, I'd like to share my thoughts and ideas with you.

Youth

I can't stress enough how much our focus must be on juveniles. We must make schools more secure, increase public school budgets, make schoolyards safe, and expand after-school programs.

My brothers and I grew up in a single-parent home, and Mom worked. If it weren't for the after-school program at P.S. 215 and the active community centers (for me, it was the JCH—the Edith and Carl Marks Jewish Community House—in Bensonhurst and the Flatbush Boys Club), I can't imagine how much trouble I'd have gotten in. We had excellent teachers whose involvement extended well after classroom hours.

While writing this book, I saw a lot of despair and hopelessness in the neighborhoods I visited. When people lose hope, they lose their values, the value of life itself, and the value of doing the right thing.

If you give kids hope early, making the school environment great by enlisting highly qualified teachers and administrators and ensuring that the school and surrounding area are safe, the positive results will be apparent.

Knowing their kids are safe and have access to an after-school program with tutoring gives parents, especially single parents, more peace of mind and a chance to concentrate on what they need to be doing, even to stay afloat.

Of course, programs cost money, but they help keep kids on track. If you don't want kids to commit crimes, give them a safe opposite direction. Investing in these kids is an investment in the community and in public safety.

In the communities I visited, it's doubtful whether those safe places exist. Play in the park? The parks are occupied by drug addicts, dealers, and gangs. Some parks are closed before dark. Where are you going to go?

We must look at school programs, schoolyards, and the schools themselves. If you want to cut down on crime, one effective way is to provide a more appealing alternative before kids even consider crime as an option.

The anchors of a neighborhood should be schools, houses of worship, and community centers.

Respect

Police, like everyone else, want to be respected, whether they're right or wrong. The simple fact is, to get respect, you have to give respect. If the police want to be community leaders—and they should want to be—they need to lead with love and respect for the whole community. I'm not just talking about captains and chiefs; I'm talking about every cop.

When police officers consider themselves to be "other," rather than part of the community, the community responds the same way. That's how cops come to be seen as an occupying force, as invaders. But when the police lead with empathy and compassion, respect follows. If you want to make a difference in a neighborhood, you need to use an entrepreneurial approach. Entrepreneurs take their place as part of the scene and utilize common sense in dealing with people. Common sense, in this instance, means empathy.

When a police officer takes someone else's perspective and thinks about what it might be like to live in a two-bedroom apartment with ten other people or to live in daily poverty with the restrictions that some people have, they develop empathy instead of thinking exclusively about being right or wrong.

Right or wrong doesn't work in this area. You can't police strictly by the law because many people don't prioritize the law. Policing with commonality, with empathy, creates a common ground and builds shared respect between the police and the public they are meant to serve and protect.

The Numbers

In New York City and Syracuse alone, police department rosters are down 25 to 30 percent in just a few years. This can't be by mistake, and it's concerning.

Is it a budgeting issue or attrition? We have more people going out the back door by way of retirement than we have coming in the front door via recruiting, and that's because the optics of becoming a police officer are not good. What needs to happen is a shift in perception—how the public views law enforcement as a career—a steady, nationwide campaign promoting police work.

The military has been doing this for decades, using commercials, print, billboards, and recruiters to attract civilians. We're shown the good that the armed services are doing protecting our nation. We pause for a minute during sporting events to honor them.

Why aren't we pausing to pay tribute to the police and firefighters and teachers? We need to do that. There's been a little more promotion of the teaching profession over the past few years (although teachers are still underpaid). Still, you never see positive stories about policing or the selflessness exhibited by police and firefighters. No one is out there emphasizing the importance of becoming a police officer or how awesome police work can be.

How about a budget set aside by the federal government and individual states to run commercials and PR promotions showing all the good that police officers do? We can't just be afraid of a few anti-police people just because they're the loudest voices in the room. It's essential to pay attention to the optics, which is how the public views policing. Unfortunately, optics isn't really what the police do well. Cops don't shine a light on themselves and say, "Look what we just did!" Someone needs to get good at it. Policing was once an attractive field of endeavor, a calling. We need that again. All those commercials about the Army and the Marines? We're paying for those. It's tax dollars. Why isn't there a budget to promote the police?

Besides the low numbers of police coming in, we're losing older officers rapidly, causing us to have very young police departments. That's dangerous. We need older officers to stay on and mentor the younger ones.

Age is particularly a problem when it comes to domestic and juvenile issues. When you have a twenty-two-year-old cop who's never had kids dealing with juveniles or family violence, it's not the same as having a forty-year-old cop who's been married and has kids.

Here's an idea: *incentivize*. When officers have worked their twenty years, give them an option. Stay for twenty-five years, collect their pension, and get rehired for up to another ten pensionable years if they choose. Collect both pension and pay. It's not my original idea. The chief in Syracuse mentioned it to me, and the Los Angeles Police Department has a similar program in place. A retired cop can stay on the job and provide younger cops with wisdom and experience instead of taking some private security job.

Visibility

There must be a more significant push to get cops back to walking a beat. Beat cops used to be part of the fabric of a community. Both Judge Solomon and Brownsville community leader Lisa Kenner favor and suggest the idea of returning cops to the beat. When a police officer walks the neighborhood, the citizens learn their name, and the officer gets to know the citizens. Cops in cars provide coverage but don't fit into the scene like cops on the beat.

Domestic Violence

On every ride-along I went on, 35 to 40 percent of the 911 calls received were reports of domestic violence. When a detective tells me he works 300 domestic violence cases a year, that's a sign that we don't have domestic violence under control and that, in many cases, intimate partners living together is dysfunctional.

It's foolish to ignore this trend, if for no other reason than economics. Once the police are summoned to a domestic violence call, someone is either going to the hospital for a psychiatric evaluation or going to jail. That's an ambulance, an emergency room bill, possibly an overnight stay in a cell, a public defender, a court case . . . the costs mount.

Funds should be allocated for community services, counseling, and help with domestic issues.

The current way of dealing with domestic issues puts tremendous pressure on the police. How do you train police, especially young officers, to deal with a forty-year-old couple fighting with each other?

In affluent communities, when couples fight, they generally don't call the police. They call a therapist—because they can afford it. Instead of spending the money on making these events a legal matter, we need to make relationship counseling available to people who can't afford it. We're already spending the money—it needs to be reallocated.

Wearing my bullet-proof vest in a holding cell.

Medical care has been shifting from emergency rooms to urgent care centers; how about urgent mental health centers?

If we are getting more serious about mental health in this country, we need to get serious everywhere, including in less affluent areas. When the police take the place of mental health providers, they're not effective because they're not trained, *it's not their job*, and it takes them away from doing their job. I'd like to see ten therapists in the 46th Precinct so people with domestic issues have someone to talk to other than the cops.

The City of New York recently instituted the Behavioral Health Emergency Assistance Response Division (B-HEARD) program. It's a good start, with teams of health professionals, including EMTs/paramedics from the fire department and mental health professionals from NYC Health + Hospitals, responding to 911 mental health calls. That takes some of the burden off the police, and it's more helpful to those in crisis.

Morale

Police stations in New York City are beat-up and run-down. I'm not sure how it is in the rest of the United States, but I'd guess that in many urban areas, sprucing up a cop shop is not a priority.

A police station that's a dump is a bad look for the public. There needs to be, in every police station, a nice, comfortable room where people who live in the neighborhood can meet with police officers and feel at ease. A clean, shiny environment sends a message about how the police feel about the community and themselves. It doesn't have to be the Taj Mahal, but police stations should look like humans work there and citizens are welcome.

On a related note, the holding cells I've seen in the precincts I've visited are subhuman. I'm not saying that people who commit crimes should be kept in luxury, but these cells should be properly maintained.

A few of the cells I've seen in the Bronx

Police stations need to look professional, orderly, and clean, not just for the public but for the officers and staff who work in them. Older precinct houses need to be rehabilitated.

Law enforcement groups from around the country come to New York City to learn from the NYPD because they're *that* good. After all, they are called New York's Finest. But the look and physical presence don't match the quality of policing. In the business world, I say you can't build a million-dollar result with minimum-wage execution.

Giving credit where it's due, the New York City Police Foundation has done an excellent job making improvements: fixing up the gyms in police stations so that officers have a pleasant place to exercise, replacing side windows in police vehicles with bulletproof glass, and other enhancements most of us never hear about. Still, everyone deserves a clean, pleasant workplace that isn't a dump, and precincts need to be improved overall.

Another morale issue is the difficulty police now have arresting individuals and getting them to stay arrested. It has to be frustrating for police officers to arrest the same individuals over and over again, only to find them back on the street almost immediately.

At some point, the laws need to be adjusted. Individuals with ten, fifteen, and twenty arrests should be treated differently than first-timers. Rearresting is expensive for taxpayers, and it's taxing and demoralizing for the officers.

We need to help officers navigate a legal system that seems to favor the offender. Maybe we need to find a way to level the playing field.

Leadership Training

The NYPD has implemented a leadership course, which I'm involved with as a lecturer, to teach leadership principles to newly promoted officers. But I don't think that's enough. The principles of leadership work at every level to improve critical thinking, decision-making, and self-discipline. Therefore, leadership training should be for everyone, top to bottom, not just when individuals move into leadership roles. Leadership principles at every level help avoid foolish errors. The best way to manage any staff is to teach them to manage themselves.

When you increase knowledge throughout the department, you'll find that officers can help other officers avoid stupid mistakes.

Training, particularly leadership training, should be a constant throughout a police career. Many of the officers I talked to have been on the job for over ten years and haven't had any training other than what they got at the Academy. Given the frequent changes in the law and police procedures, that's just not enough.

Communication

One of the most amazing things I learned on this journey is the astonishing amount and quality of verbal communication among police officers necessary to get the job done. Verbal communication—not texting, not social media interactions, but people *talking to each other*. The communication with Central and among officers on patrol is clear and precise, sometimes at a granular level. Everybody knows what's going on, whether it be a particular incident or what's happening in the city, and communication among all the precincts and leadership is incredibly efficient and effective.

That level of communication is a big part of why the NYPD is one of the best police departments in the world, and many other organizations can learn a lot from it. Not all communication is equal; there is nothing like clear, crisp, consistent verbal communication. Cops on patrol in NYC are in constant contact with each other. What goes over the radio, between a patrol car and Central and between patrol cars, is brief and concise, but it's transparent and two-way, and everyone involved understands each other. Most current forms of communication have value, whether email or Slack or whatever, but nothing replaces spoken conversation. One big reason we have such a highly committed police force is that individual officers are included in the conversations, and they know what's going on. When people are trusted to know and understand, that breeds commitment, whether you're a cop, a businessperson, or a Little League coach.

In addition to that level of communication is a level of dedication. I didn't see police officers concerned about who got credit for an arrest. I didn't see cops slacking because they were "just" backup. I saw the guys in the fourth car arrive on the scene with the same intense commitment as the first guys. I saw a fellowship of officers who had each other's backs.

Everything was a group effort. And on the return to the precinct house, the desk sergeant knew what had happened because the communication had been thorough.

We need more of that kind of solid connection in all our relationships.

Defund? Are You Nuts?

When I started researching for this book, I wanted to learn more about what was right and wrong about urban policing. Here at the end of the book, I hope I've increased your awareness and perhaps inspired you to learn more for yourself.

The police and the community need a lot of assistance, and maybe instead of asking, "Why should I care?" we should ask, "How can I help?"

In the past few years, we've all heard calls to defund the police—that is, to redirect funding away from the police department to other government agencies. That might be an understandable overreaction to terrible events, but one has to be highly misinformed or even completely uninformed to even think about defunding the police.

Saying we don't need a strong police force is like saying we don't need food. Saying the police need less funding is like saying we need less air to breathe.

Most people don't realize the costs of crime and the expenses of keeping us safe. We need to get in tune with the police and with the people who live in our communities and help both sides.

I hope this book helps promote an understanding of both the police and the residents of our neighborhoods. Neither group is bad. We need to work together to lift each other up.

The End, and hopefully the Beginning . . .

Acknowledgments

I couldn't have written this book alone, and there are quite a few individuals whose assistance deserves appreciation.

I owe a debt of gratitude to K. C. Fuchs, CEO of the Silver Shield Foundation, who introduced me to the NYPD. I also want to thank the leadership at One Police Plaza for granting me access to the precincts, the Academy, and the Crime Lab.

There are many members of the police, both in New York City and in Syracuse, who helped make this book happen. I'm grateful to each one of them.

I particularly want to offer my thanks to:

Inspector John Potkay, Captain Rebecca BukofzerTavarez, Russell Smith, Lisa Kenner, Sergeant Catherine Kunst, Officer Brian Rao, Sergeant Jamie Blandeburgo, Detective Mark Kopystianskyj, Detective Matt Brady, Captain Matt Strong, Sergeant Billy Hempstead, Lieutenant Mike Bopp, Detective Rob Bustamante, Nicholas Grenier, Captain Tamecca Greene, Officer Thomas Corcoran, Captain David Miller, Deputy Inspector Craig Edelman, Detective Bureau Assistant Chief Jason Savino, Detective Sergeant Alexander Rapp, Syracuse Deputy Chief

Mark Rusin, Judge Charles H. Solomon, Dina Denlea, Russell "Big Russ" Smith, Lisa Kenner,

And all members of law enforcement and community leaders, whether I've met them or not. Thank you for your service.

Brandon

* * *

I want to acknowledge the folks who provided editorial and design assistance: Michele Matrisciani of Bookchic LLC, as well as Gary and Carol Rosenberg, The Book Couple.

I'm also taking this opportunity to express my gratitude to my beloved wife, Lillian, for her patience, love, and support.

C. L. S.

About the Authors

Brandon Steiner is the Founder & President of The Steiner Agency, the nation's premier independent athlete procurement source, and CollectibleXchange, an online platform for fans, collectors, store owners, celebrities, athletes, and teams to buy and sell collectibles. In 1988, he founded Steiner Sports, which he built into a sports marketing powerhouse and served as CEO until 2017.

Throughout his career, Brandon has amassed success through serial entrepreneurship and marketing savvy. He is also a premier motivational and inspirational speaker, having spoken to world-class organizations such as the New York Yankees, BMW North America, Nike, Live Nation, Cornell University, TEDx, and Harvard Business School.

Brandon currently appears on the MSG+ Network and the YES Network, as well as Facebook Live and eBay Live. He has appeared frequently on CNBC, CNN, MSNBC, ESPN, and in newspapers, including the *New York Times* and the *Wall Street Journal*.

Brandon is the author of three other books: *The Business Playbook; You Gotta Have Balls: How a Kid from Brooklyn Started from Scratch, Bought Yankee Stadium, and Created a Sports Empire;* and *Living on Purpose: Stories About Faith, Fortune, and Fitness that Will Lead You to an Extraordinary Life.*

Brandon bleeds Syracuse Orange. He lives in Scarsdale, New York, with his wife, Mara.

To connect with Brandon, visit his website, *BrandonSteiner.com*. There, you can subscribe to his *What Else?* blog.

To connect on social media:

Facebook: facebook.com/steiner

Instagram: @BrandonSteiner

X (formerly Twitter): @BrandonSteiner

LinkedIn: linkedin.com/in/BrandonSteiner

C. L. [Cary] Steiner is a professional ghostwriter, editor, and freelance writer. He also writes an online column titled *I'm Not Complaining* [https://notcomplaining.beehiiv.com].

Cary lives in Cornelius, North Carolina, with his wife, Lillian, and Peanut the Elderly Wonder Dog. He has, happily, no social media presence.

You can contact Cary at clsteiner@duck.com

Made in the USA
Columbia, SC
10 July 2025

7302e6d4-741a-4f9c-9eda-558cab054570R01